What's the best way to handle feedback (good and bad) in our first performance reviews?
—ASKED AT GOLDMAN SACHS

What makes a great cover letter (or do we not need them anymore), and what kinds of résumés stand out for you?
—ASKED AT NBC

What are ideal first steps for girls interested in writing shows for TV and film?
—ASKED AT DISNEY

Is working here your dream job? If not, what is?
—ASKED AT YOUTUBE

Why is it so important to be really prepared, or even overprepared, for every single meeting?
—ASKED AT NINE WEST WITH TYRA BANKS

What specific skills are most important to be great in your job, and did you always have them?
—ASKED AT VIACOMCBS

THE EPIC MENTOR GUIDE

INSIDER ADVICE FOR GIRLS EYEING THE WORKFORCE FROM 180 BOSS WOMEN WHO KNOW

ILLANA RAIA
FOUNDER OF ÊTRE

The Epic Mentor Guide
Insider Advice for Girls Eyeing the Workforce from 180 Boss Women Who Know

Published by Forefront Books.

Cover Design by Bruce Gore, Gore Studio, Inc.
Back Cover Design by Jennifer Vance, Books Forward
Interior Design by Linda Bourdeaux, thedesigndesk.com

ISBN: 978-1-63763-049-5 print
ISBN: 978-1-63763-050-1 e-book

TABLE OF MENTORS

FOREWORD

Mentors have helped me throughout my career and life, and I've been blessed to have many who continue to offer me advice, encouragement, and guidance. So when Illana told me about *The Epic Mentor Guide* and the 180 boss women who contributed, I was intrigued and excited.

As CEO at Worth, knowing your self-worth was something we talked about a lot with the Women and Worth Community. I saw firsthand from the girls at Être the impact mentoring had on their confidence, energy, and growth. They developed by just being in the same room, asking questions and listening to inspiring female leaders share their stories—many of whom are featured in this book. What did those girls and the female leaders have in common? Determination and the courage to go after their dreams and make a positive impact in the world.

Illana's book shows how, by simply asking questions and being curious, you can provide an epic guide to life that, quite frankly, anyone looking for career advice and wisdom should read.

—JULIET SCOTT-CROXFORD
President, North America, Brompton Bicycle, Former CEO of Worth

INTRODUCTION

Five years ago, when I launched a mentorship platform for girls called Être, my idea was to bring girls face-to-face with female leaders where they worked. As the French name suggests, I wanted to help girls figure out who they wanted *to be*.

Immediately after Être's first visit inside a company (cue the cheering for Spotify), girls who heard about the event started asking: *Wait, what did everyone in the room ask? What did the women answer? What's one thing the execs wanted girls to know?*

The more we relayed the answers, the faster new questions came in. *If you go to NBC and visit* Saturday Night Live, *please ask this . . . ! If you meet women on Wall Street, I've always wondered . . .*

So we kept asking.

And during every visit—whether onstage at YouTube, in the cafeteria at Google, in front of Geena Davis, or on the floor of the New York Stock Exchange—girls shot their hands up to ask smart questions. They'd confidently look icons like Tyra Banks straight in the eye, or chat casually with execs from Disney or *Billboard* over Zoom, and let their curiosity run wild:

How did you know you'd be good at your job? What's more important in your role: passion or persistence? Is it weird to be the only woman on your team? Is this your dream job? No? What would be?

And watching from the back of the room or Zoom, I inevitably had the same thought: *How could girls everywhere get to ask these questions?* Quickly followed by: *Because every woman would probably answer.*

That's how this book came about. Because of your questions.

As girls like you moved through high school and college, eyeing internships and finding first jobs, the questions grew more specific:

How do I land an internship at SpaceX? What makes a LinkedIn profile stand out? What can I actually ask in an interview? Can I use TikTok to network?

You asked, so we asked.

And 180 phenomenal women answered.

Wondering what it's like to be the first female coach or general manager of any men's professional sports team? Ask Nancy Lieberman or Kim Ng.

Want to know what Veronica Beard thinks you should wear to work, how Dawn Porter went from practicing law to making movies with Oprah, or what Bobbi Brown wants you to do when you hear the word *no* at work? We did too.

Listen to what Hoda Kotb thinks about resilience, why Dylan Lauren opened a candy store, how the CEO of Headspace can help you stay mindful, and what TheSkimm's founders want to tell you about transcending the trap of expectations. Concerned about negotiating your first salary raise? Who better to ask than The Fair Pay Act's Lilly Ledbetter?

Answering girls' questions about diversity and inclusion, raising hands, speaking up and standing out, *The Epic Mentor Guide* is your inside track to the workforce before you get there. Because sometimes it's better to know what's coming even before you start.

It's your career path, so drive the guide any way you want—move through the Table of Mentors alphabetically, search for companies and industries you love in the index, or open randomly to a brand-new role model or question that resonates.

A word about the questions you'll see: Some appear in their original form (exactly as they were asked in a boardroom or slid into our DMs), and some represent a compilation of different, but related, inquiries. Where we saw a topic trending, we condensed multiple questions into one to be able to ask the right mentor. The names of the girls who contributed questions are noted at the end of the book, and they rule.

A word about the mentors you'll meet: Oh, these women. Role models, champions, and rock stars one and all. If we define a mentor as someone who takes an active interest in your future, someone who invests her time and energy to bolster your confidence, challenge your assumptions, and inspire next steps, then you hold in your hands 180 gold star mentors.

All of these women were once in your shoes, seeking advice as they

entered the workforce. And all of them have epic wisdom to share. Most of them, when they responded to our questions, said *"Oh my God, I wish I had this when I was starting out."*

I look at this book as just the beginning. It's called *The Epic Mentor Guide*—not *The Ultimate Mentor Guide*—because there are so many more mentors to meet, industries to investigate, and questions to ask.

So jump in, read up, and keep those hands raised. Every leader in this book gave us her favorite social media handle, so you can keep learning from these role models in real time. Want mentors who not only walk the walk, but want you to follow in their footsteps?

They're right here.

Keep your questions coming and we'll keep asking today's leaders for answers. Because the workforce is changing. And mentors—whether they are in your office, across the globe, or on the page—matter right now.

You're building a future. We're building a pipeline.

I can't wait to see what happens next.

XO,

Illana

"IT'S NEVER TOO EARLY TO ENVISION WHAT YOU COULD BE, AND IT'S NEVER TOO LATE TO REALIZE YOUR GOALS. KEEP REINVENTING YOURSELF."

—LINDA FARBER POST
Nurse, Sculptor, Writer, Lawyer, Medical Ethicist,
and the Author's Mother

What is your advice for girls

who are committed to their

sports and want to start

prepping for the Olympics?

"

First—*what* do you want to achieve in your sport?
Dig deep and really understand what it is that you want
your legacy to be. *Then* commit with your entire heart,
soul, and body to achieve that. Look at yourself in the
mirror and be honest—was that session the best I could do?
Did I give *everything* I had today? Be kind to yourself,
but be thorough—leave no stone unturned. *When* there's
a day you don't feel like training—and there will be plenty—
picture your goal and legacy, and remember *why* you
started this crazy journey to become an Olympian.

Don't give up! The road isn't going to be easy,
and it probably won't look like the road you envisioned—
but the journey can be the most life-changing experience.
Representing your country on the world stage is an
experience not many girls get to do!

—ABBEY WILLCOX
Freestyle Aerial Skier
ABBEYWILLCOX

1

What are the initial questions girls should ask themselves when thinking about scaling their first big idea?

"

The first thing girls should ask themselves
when thinking about scaling their first big idea is: *Why?*
Why does this matter to me? Girls are drowning in a
culture of comparison today, but our lifeboat is our *why*,
which allows us to move away from operating in the fear
that we are not good enough to knowing we are
and operating in the power of believing that.

When we are connected to our why—how we think about
ourselves, the energy we put out into the universe, what we
create, our decisions, the steps we take—all align with the
wonderful essence of who we were created to be and what we
can accomplish. That is where every girl's power lives and
where ideas aren't just ideas, they become magic
that we collectively benefit from.

— ALEX BATDORF
CEO of Getting Sh!t Done
GETSHITDONEQUEEN

2

What were the career steps

that first led you to Spotify,

and what is the coolest part

of your role now as VP

of Global Brand?

"

After leaving a comfortable role at Nike, I made a series of experimental career moves that offered a lot of perspective on both where I wanted and didn't want to spend my time. This included about a year and a half of freelance/consulting work while I figured out what my next full-time role would be. The beauty of that experience was that I said *yes* to jobs I wouldn't have said *yes* to because they were temporary. While I didn't know it at the time, that was career-experience *gold*, and led me to accept a temporary role at Spotify, which has evolved eight years later into my current role as VP of Global Brand. The coolest part of my current role is hands-down the opportunity to lead a team of the most talented and creative, young, culturally connected people in the world— and in doing the work we do, we get to create work for, and alongside, some of the most culturally resonant artists and creators of our time.

—ALEXANDRA TANGUAY
VP of Global Brand at Spotify
LINKEDIN.COM/IN/ALEXANDRAT

3

How did you battle imposter syndrome

while building Bulletin, and what is your advice on

this to girls starting out in the work world?

"

To face my impostor syndrome head-on, I started
keeping a tally of all the things I had accomplished that
once felt so impossible to me. I'd write them down in the
Notes section of my phone or in a journal. Success
is built on baby steps, not a swell of work or lineup
of accomplishments that come in all at once.
I think logging those baby steps and taking
pride in them is very important.

— ALI KRIEGSMAN
Cofounder and COO of Bulletin
ALIKRIEGS

4

What is your advice for girls looking to break into broadcast journalism today—what college majors, internships, or activities do you think are most important?

The key is networking! Ask every journalism professor you have for their contacts in the field. Get a hands-on internship—one where you get to do actual reporting—and network with everyone working there. Stay in touch with them; have them introduce you to colleagues they know. Meet as many journalists as you can, and soon you'll be connected to people with the power to hire you.

—ALISYN CAMEROTA
CNN Anchor
 ALISYNCAMEROTA

How did the mentorship you received change as you rose through the ranks on Wall Street, and what advice would you give to entrepreneurial girls who dream about ringing the NYSE bell someday?

"

Senior mentors became harder to find as I progressed in my career on Wall Street, so I found a replacement: my own employees. I learned that if I surrounded myself with people who were always willing to tell me the truth— and I encouraged them to do so with an open door and an open mind—I would grow and learn from their guidance.

Do not let anyone allow you to believe that your business will fail. Every entrepreneur overcame obstacles. Look toward the bell podium and away from the naysayers.

—AMANDA HINDLIAN
Global Head of Capital Markets at the NYSE
 LINKEDIN.COM/IN/AMANDA-HINDLIAN-BB23584

6

How does your role as an art and archaeology conservator utilize your STEM skills, and what is one piece of advice you would pass on to girls seeking to enter this field today?

"

Conservators rely on a foundational knowledge of chemistry and fine art. In order for us to know how best to restore damaged areas of an artwork or prevent them from degrading, we must first know the chemical compositions of pigments or other materials because different compositions require different treatment methods, chemicals, and analysis techniques—a wrong treatment could result in new or further damage.

My advice to aspiring conservators is to study chemistry, understand that great patience is required in this field, and know that there are always people who want to see you succeed and will help if you ask.

—AMANDA IMAI
Art and Archaeological Conservator
CURATORIALCHRONICLES

7

Why do you think it is important for girls to stay in hockey, and what lifelong skills do you think sticking with your sport provides?

"

When it comes to career and personal development, I believe the key to succeeding is your ability to be consistent. During my National Team career, we learned about the importance of 'aggregation of marginal gains,' which means your drive to get 1 percent better every day. Over time, these percentages grow into bigger sums. Consistency is the driving force behind change.

—AMANDA PELKEY
Olympic Gold Medalist – USA Hockey
PELKEY21

How do you use your engineering degree in your job at LEGO, and what would you tell creative girls today about finding jobs that combine their interests in engineering, play, and design?

"

The greatest tool you can ever equip yourself with is creativity. It may seem small, but when you train it, it can give you the confidence to take on even the biggest challenge. I never dreamed my studies in engineering and design would take me where they have, but there are so many awesome jobs out there if you take a look around, so dream big and find something that makes you smile every day!

—AMY CORBETT
Design Lead at LEGO
BRICKMASTERAMY

In what ways do you see

the global modeling industry

becoming more diverse, and what do you want

aspiring young models to remember before

each casting call?

"

Fashion has the potential to destigmatize and celebrate all bodies by including them in the narrative of beauty. The modeling industry has been forced to make some critical changes, which we hope signifies a new era for modeling. For aspiring models, self-care is as crucial to your success as the agency you are signed to. Remember rejection is part of the job, so surround yourself with positive people, be kind to yourself, stay true to yourself, and don't compare yourself to others.

Models change as often as trends so avoid taking the industry too seriously and become confident enough to be your own unique self.

—Angel Sinclair
Founder of Models of Diversity
MODELSOFDIVERSITY

10

> Does "grit" have different definitions, depending on how old you are, and is grit the most important skill to have when starting first jobs?

Grit is probably not as important as honesty, but it is important. A young adult who is gritty is eagerly pursuing career options that align with their developing interests and values, and does so with a daily dedication to feedback and improvement, and resilience in the face of (inevitable) setbacks.

—ANGELA DUCKWORTH
Founder and CEO of The Character Lab,
Author of GRIT, and Professor at the University of Pennsylvania
🐦 ANGELADUCKW

11

How has TikTok changed the way global brands tell their stories and interact with customers, and do you have any general advice to girls eyeing careers in digital marketing?

"

TikTok has transformed the connection between brands and people to a deeper, more authentic experience that is 'full funnel,' meaning a brand can now go from being discovered for the first time to purchased and loved within a day.

My advice to aspiring digital marketers is to embrace change as a fundamental part of this career. Truly great digital marketers are able to flex multiple skill sets and consistently adapt to the new platforms and technologies that arise every year.
That's what makes it fun!

—ANISHA RAGHAVAN
CMO, Global Brands Americas at Walgreens Boots Alliance
LINKEDIN.COM/IN/ANISHARAGHAVAN

12

How can girls entering the workforce

for the first time incorporate UN Global Goals

into their personal professional goals and

help embed them in workplace culture?

" "

We won't reach gender equality without workplace equality. Seek out and create gender-equal workplaces— those that are eliminating gender pay gaps, ensuring gender equality in leadership, supporting women-owned businesses, and speaking out about the need for change. Standing up for a feminist workplace won't just empower you, but will create opportunities for countless others too.

—ANITA BHATIA
Assistant Secretary-General and
Deputy Executive Director, UN Women
in LINKEDIN.COM/IN/BHATIA95

13

What did it feel like to report the news

on camera for the first time, and what advice

do you have for girls who want on-camera

careers in journalism?

I remember the first day I was 'live' on the air; it was an out-of-body experience seeing the red light go on in the studio. The trick to being a good newscaster is to be as conversational as possible, like you're talking to one person, not a whole audience. Once you master the 'talking to a good friend in the backyard,' naturalness comes through. An audience wants to see a real person.

—Ann Nyberg
WTNH8 News Anchor
ⓘ ANNNYBERG

What is your advice

to girls embarking on first jobs

or internships, specifically regarding building

big lives on their own terms from day one?

"

You have so much to offer the world, but those first few jobs aren't going to be your dream job. You are there to learn how work works (and pay your bills!). Pay attention to how your boss commands a room. Watch how ideas get pitched and greenlighted. Listen to the way the people around you work with each other—both with their bosses and the people who report to them. This is all laying the foundation for your ideas to get heard, for you to build your team, for you to create a life and a career on your terms.

—ANN SHOKET
Founder of New Power Media,
Leader of TheLi.st, and Author of THE BIG LIFE
[O] ANNSHOKET

15

How did you go from medical school to NASA, and what surprised you most during your 192 hours in space?

"

I wanted to be an astronaut from the time I was twelve years old listening to Alan Shepard's historic launch in May 1961. Of course it didn't seem like a realistic goal, as all the astronauts at that time were male and test pilots, a career path not available to women at that time. As I pursued my higher education, I decided to combine my love of math and science with my desire to help people and decided to go to medical school. In the back of my mind, I was hoping that even if I could not become an astronaut, perhaps I could be a doctor on a space station or a moon base.

In early June of 1977, as I was completing my internship, I found out quite by accident that NASA was looking for not only pilot astronauts but mission specialist or scientist astronauts as well. I applied (making the deadline by one day) and in January 1978 found out that I had been selected for the first class of space shuttle astronauts, the largest, most diverse class of astronauts that NASA had ever selected and the first six women. It was my dream come true and the culmination of years of hard work. I became a member of the TFNGs (Thirty-Five New Guys) and flew onboard the space shuttle *Discovery* November 8–16, 1984—becoming the first mother in space.

Our mission was bold and exciting, the first to rescue two communication satellites and return them to Earth. There were few surprises due to our excellent training, but I was surprised (which makes sense when you think about it) to watch meteors enter the Earth's atmosphere below us. It was the adventure of a lifetime and a childhood dream come true. Follow your dreams and don't give up.

—ANNA FISHER
Chemist, Physician, Retired NASA Astronaut, and the First Mom in Space
🄾 NASA

16

"

What are three things you want aspiring

female chefs to know about finding—

and crushing—their dream jobs?

"

Show up and be committed to doing your job well.
Be prepared and do research outside of work if you need to.

You don't need to be the loudest voice in the room, but be the strongest.
Be reasonable, rational, and empathetic. But also, don't take any sh*t.

Own yourself, love what you do, and have a sense of humor! It's infectious!
It makes other people happy to work with you—and for you.

—ANNE BURRELL
Chef, Food Network Personality, and Author
@CHEFANNEBURRELL

17

Can your first job prepare you to be CEO?

"

My first job was at PepsiCo. I was fortunate to be in their Management
Training Program, where I had the opportunity to learn from the ground up.
My first assignment was route sales representative. I was given a sales territory and
the objective was to grow revenue and delight customers. I had my own eighteen-
foot truck. I loaded the truck myself each day and worked hard at selling displays and
stocking the shelves. My first leadership role at PepsiCo was a district sales leader.
I managed fifteen route sales representatives who were twice my age,
all members of the Teamsters Union. I was the only women and
was quickly reminded I was younger than their daughters.

My first leadership role taught me great lessons that I still leverage today.
It continues to help me in my role as CEO of Wella Company. (1) Stand in
Their Shoes—really listen to the needs of the team. I had the opportunity to get to
know all fifteen of them. It enabled me to motivate them to succeed. (2) Respect Is
Earned; It's Not a Title—these amazing men had twenty-plus years of experience.
I learned early on, getting their respect was showing how I could add value. Working
hard and helping them achieve their financial and personal goals earned their respect.
(3) Teamwork Is Dreamwork—each person on the team had something they were
good at. They worked as individuals, but not as a team. Leveraging their
best practices and matriculating amongst the team allowed them to perform
collectively at their peak. They won every sales contest during my tenure.

—ANNIE YOUNG-SCRIVNER
CEO of Wella Company
 LINKEDIN.COM/IN/ANNIE-YOUNG-SCRIVNER-B670B614

18

" What does "leaning in" mean to you, and

what is one piece of advice you received through

an all-female network that you would pass

on to girls starting first jobs?

"

Leaning in means imagining your biggest, boldest life
and then going after it unapologetically.

My career advice?
Always ask—if you don't ask for what you want, you'll never get it.

—ARCHANA GILRAVI
Vice President, Partnerships at LeanIn.org
in LINKEDIN.COM/IN/ARCHANARAVICHANDRAN

19

What is something you want girls to know about the automotive logistics industry, and what are the two most important pieces of mentor advice you have ever received?

"

While the stereotype may seem extremely male-dominated, it has made huge strides becoming a surprisingly welcoming environment for female leaders. Many associate leadership qualities with masculine characteristics—especially in this industry; however, you do not need to sacrifice femininity for another's approval of the path to your success.

(1) Be yourself, unapologetically, and (2) Fear and weaknesses are not indicators of what you need to run from, but indicators of where you need to grow. Run *toward* your fears aggressively and with calculated intention.

— ARIA TACTAQUIN
Assistant Vice President,
Business Development at RCG Logistics
in LINKEDIN.COM/IN/ARIA-TACTAQUIN

20

> What are transferable skills, and why are they important for girls new to the workforce to understand?

In our new normal, your transferable skills give you a competitive advantage. Skills that you demonstrate in your job, volunteer activities, classes, or entrepreneurial pursuits are visible to those around you. When you embark on conversations related to a job search or career change, skill-based networking is critical. Your professional networks will provide feedback on your candidacy for a role based on those moments where your skills stood out to them.

—Asha Aravindakshan
Author of SKILLS: THE COMMON DENOMINATOR
DCASHA

21

Why are the strategies you learn in chess so useful in other areas of life . . . particularly in the work world?

"

The strategies we learn in chess don't only teach us how to *solve* problems, but they teach us how to *find* problems, come up with various solutions to move forward, and decide where to go next effectively and quickly. On and off the chessboard, on the field or off the field, or in the office and out, young women need to be able to visualize their goal and create a path to get there. It's all about life skills!

—ASHLEY LYNN PRIORE
Founder of The Queen's Gambit
ASHLEYLYNNPRIORE

22

How did you combine your passions for sports and education when you launched insideLINES, and what advice would you give today's girls thinking about pursuing jobs in podcasting?

"

Sports and education go hand in hand. Be open to learning and educating yourself in order to expand your knowledge base and grow. This not only applies to sports but also business. It is imperative to not only do your research in podcasting, but also adapt in an ever-changing world of media.

Believe in yourself and gather the courage to ask questions to people in your field. It is extremely beneficial to learn from veterans or mentors willing to pay it forward because they have the experience and will likely save you from making the same costly mistakes they've made in the past. Those are called angels on Earth. Always thank them and be cognizant of opportunities for you to do the same for others when the time arrives.

—ATOYA BURLESON
Founder of insideLINES Podcast
ATOYABURLESON

When is the right time to protect
a big idea with a patent, and do
you have any advice for innovative
girls entering that process?

"

The best time to protect the big idea with a patent is as soon as you can describe it as new and useful. In America, the United States Patent and Trademark Office uses a 'first to file' system. So, if you are first to file, you have the advantage right away. Of course, the best big ideas to file on have already also been vetted with a search that shows what has been done like this in the past around your idea. Above all, the big idea has to be new.

To begin this you need to be able to tell the story of how your idea is new and why it is needed and different from past patented ideas. Then you keep to that known truth as your patent application gets examined before it can become a granted patent. Odds are not too many people have seen the solution from your eyes, so if your idea solves a new problem—it could be a new idea. Don't get discouraged if you have to twist and turn it a bit to make it 'newer' and 'more different' compared to the work from others . . . that's what the art of creation is all about!

— AUDREY SHERMAN
3M's "100 Patent Woman"
in LINKEDIN.COM/IN/AUDREYASHERMAN

24

How can girls get their true selves noticed by colleges, and are there particular tips you have for girls applying from outside the US?

"

As I discuss in my book *GET REAL AND GET IN,* students often get swept up in the 'impressiveness paradox.' They're trying (too hard) to stand out to their top choice colleges and failing to understand and live up to their own values. Applicants owe it to themselves to get real: What kind of college experience and life do they want? How can they define and stay true to that vision, despite well-meaning adults who are quick to offer ideas about what they should want and how they should represent themselves?

When applying, stick to your clear vision for what you want out of college, and make sure it is well-articulated throughout your application and that your ideas for what you want to do are corroborated by experiences you've already had. If you're applying from outside of the US, make sure to discuss what purpose and meaning studying abroad would afford you and what value you would add.

—Dr. Aviva Legatt
Educational Consultant and Author of GET REAL AND GET IN
AVIVALEGATT

What is the best part about creating and producing shows for Disney Junior, and what are ideal first steps for girls interested in pursuing a similar career path?

"

I love creating characters that empower and inspire kids as well as adults and showcasing worlds and storylines that have a lasting impact on kids and their families. *MIRA, ROYAL DETECTIVE,* an animated mystery-adventure series that I developed and am producing, is inspired by the cultures and customs of India and follows the smart, brave, and resourceful Mira, who is appointed to the role of royal detective by the Queen. In developing this series, my deepest mission is to bring strong, diverse characters to the forefront, and partnering with Disney Junior has been a joy in realizing this goal.

For girls interested in pursuing the career path of writing and producing, I think it's important to give a lot of thought to the types of stories you want told and characters you want to see on the screen. Writing is a craft and takes a lot of practice and time to nurture. The magic of storytelling comes when you can express your unique point of view to the world. Dig deep. What themes speak to you? What do you have to say that is your deepest truth?

— BECCA TOPOL
Series Developer/Producer and Head Writer at Disney
TOPOLBECCA

How do we find balance in new careers?
How do we excel in new jobs without
sacrificing our actual lives?

"

Your career will take on a life of its own, and it's yours. Life happens. Live your life—or your bosses, increased responsibilities, and what seems really important at the time will live it for you. Be true to yourself. Own your life. Own your worth.

—BETH O'CONNELL
Former Executive Producer, NBC News; Former Editor-In-Chief, UBS Client Strategy Office; and Être Advisor
LINKEDIN.COM/IN/ELIZABETHOCONNELL1

27

What would you tell girls eyeing professional sports today who are breaking their own barriers?

66

I'd tell them to love themselves. Affirm that love on a daily basis so that you are unwavering as you maneuver through life, personally and professionally. Never fear putting yourself out of your comfort zone; that's where the most growth comes. And lastly, live in the moment, because they come and go extremely fast. Smile and laugh often; don't sweat the small stuff!

—BLAKE BOLDEN
First Black Player to Compete in the NWHL and First Black Female (and Second Woman Ever) NHL Scout
 SPORTBLAKE

What do you want girls starting in the work world to remember when they hear the word *no*?

"

No one likes to be told *no*, so give yourself a
minute to breathe and process it. Then, turn the
no into an 'I can.' Start to think of a new plan—
find a different door, and if you can't find a door,
look for a window. Sometimes it's the sign to do
something completely different. Be diligent
and trust your next move.

—BOBBI BROWN
Makeup Artist and Founder of Jones Road Beauty
JUSTBOBBIDOTCOM

Why is it still so hard for women to raise money for startups and join corporate boards, and what can those of us just joining the workforce do to change that?

"

It remains hard for women to join corporate boards because the boards (and cap tables) of private companies of all sizes are still largely male and white, and board seats are primarily filled by networking. We often don't hear about them, but advisory board positions and smaller for-profit board seats lay the foundation for the kind of networking, professional advancement, and for-profit board experience that women need in order to access the larger, sought-after corporate board opportunities down the road. And yet these opportunities are controlled almost entirely by an invisible and informal network that women are not typically a part of.

When it comes to women accessing funding, they face similar chicken-and-the-egg problems—venture capital, private equity, family offices, and other sources of funds are still largely the same demographic, which creates all sorts of implicit bias and other barriers for women founders. Women also tend to miss out on funding and growth opportunities because they don't have access to that same 'whisper network,' which often includes powerful advisors.

So, what can we do about it? We can start to 'hack' the system by creating places for women to initiate and advance their for-profit board careers, earn equity, and invest. One way to do this is by tapping into the incredible value of women entrepreneurs— we can empower women founders to build out and leverage their advisory and governing boards from the start. Bringing these two groups together creates a mutually beneficial marketplace that creates an escape hatch from the chicken-and-egg problems that have kept women from getting board seats, accruing equity, investing, and accessing funding.

—BREEN SULLIVAN
Founder of The Fourth Floor
 LINKEDIN.COM/IN/BREENSULLIVAN

30

> **As a US Senate Chamber Assistant, how did you keep your wits about you on January 6, 2021, and what do you want girls to know about staying calm when chaos hits at work?**

When chaos began on January 6, there was confusion and fear among everyone in the Capitol—especially among young staff. The one thing that never wavered that day was the support and compassion of the young women I worked with on the floor. We stuck together, escaped the Senate chamber safely, and looked after each other as the violent attack unfolded. They had my back and I had theirs—it's something I'll never forget and I encourage all young women to remember in times of panic at work or in the larger world.

—BRENNAN LEACH
Former United States Senate Chamber Assistant
BRENNANLEACH

31

What does it feel like to create images that go viral, and what is your advice to artistic girls who want to create images with meaning?

"

Creating, to me, is about communication. I try to inspire empathy where it might not have been before, and my advice to budding creatives is to do the same thing: Learn how to care deeply about yourself and other human beings, and then figure out ways to creatively express that. Focus on the story you want to tell, the emotions you feel, and the needs of your community.
Everything else is extraneous.

—Bria Goeller
Artist and Creator of the iconic
Ruby Bridges/Kamala Harris image
@BRIAGOELLER

32

What are smart steps girls today can take to enter the real estate space early, like you did, and what is one piece of mentor advice you would like to pass on to us?

“

First, take a class focusing on getting started in
real estate, to understand which asset class is right for
you and where to begin. Second, get your real estate agent
license as soon as you possibly can. It's essentially free
money when you are looking to find your own projects,
sell your own projects, and you'll know exactly how to
design them by looking at comps and understanding what
makes things valuable versus not so much. Last, join your
local Real Estate Investors Association. By doing that,
you'll get to know investors and you'll meet people who
have deals you can buy and people you can sell your deals
to. Bonus: Read *RICH DAD POOR DAD* by Robert
Kiyosaki and *THINK AND GROW RICH* by
Napoleon Hill just to get your mind right.

—BRITNIE TURNER
Force for Good Serial Entrepreneur
BRITNIETURNER

33

What kinds of leadership or teamwork lessons did you learn in space, and how can they be applied by girls entering the workforce on Earth?

"

It might seem like people achieve big goals all by
themselves. In my experience, it rarely works that way.
My advice to you is simple: Learn to recognize when you
need help and how to ask for it. And, in turn,
be sure to provide that help to others.

Filling out an application is often the doorway
to opportunity. Be brave on those applications! Share
who you are and what you bring—especially aspects of
yourself that are unexpected or unusual. You never
know what mix of skills and experience
will turn out to be just right.

—CADY COLEMAN
Retired NASA Astronaut
ASTRO_CADY

Why is being effective at work more important than being right?

> **"**
>
> Why is being effective more important than being right? While I'm not saying there is no value in being right, of course there is, the ability to see the best possible solution is a gift. That said, being right means nothing if you can't get people on board with your vision. Taking the time to understand the people you need on board in order to be successful and working together to get things over the finish line is far more important than simply being smart enough to know the right answer.
>
> It's a question of value—do you value being right? Or do you value the ability to accomplish meaningful things?

—CALLIE REYNOLDS
Chief Customer Officer of Capitolis
LINKEDIN.COM/IN/CALLIEWREYNOLDS

35

How can girls avoid getting caught in

the trap of expectations—whether being seen

as too confident or being underestimated—

in their first jobs?

"

Landing our first jobs in the media industry brought so many
feelings: a ton of excitement, a sense of relief, and a bit (OK, a
whole lot) of nervousness. With your first job, you may have the
urge to show off all of your skills right away, but it's important
to avoid getting caught in the trap of expectations.

Be confident in knowing what you know and what you don't
know. Share your knowledge and strengths with your team,
identify and work on areas where you can grow, and ask
questions with intention.

—CARLY ZAKIN AND DANIELLE WEISBERG
Cofounders of TheSkimm
 CARLYANDDANIELLE

36

What makes an environment "healthy" from an architecture and design standpoint, and how can we keep our spaces feeling calm, productive, and invigorating?

"

How we design and use space has a direct impact on our health, so remember the ABCDs of Wellness Design for every space—activity, biophilia, community, and daylight—to help keep you healthy and happy. Activity protects our bodies from the harmful effects of being sedentary, biophilia uses our evolutionary response to nature to calm our stress reactions, community helps mental health by creating belonging and connection to others, and daylight helps our internal systems the way that nature designs them to run. The ABCDs of Wellness Design can be applied to every space—give it a try!

—CAROLYN RICKARD-BRIDEAU
Partner at Little Diversified Architectural Consulting
in LINKEDIN.COM/IN/CAROLYN-RICKARD-BRIDEAU-AIA-WELL-AP-LEED-AP-BD-C-0A62221

What do you want today's girls to know about mental wellness and balance in the workplace, and why is it important to be mindful of this from the start of a new job?

Pick a company to work for whose purpose makes your heart beat stronger every day. Bring your whole self to work because your whole self is your special power. To do that, on a sustainable basis, you have to tend to your whole self, especially your mind. That way, you are improving what makes you special every day.

—CeCe Morken
CEO of Headspace
 CGMORKEN

At Sears, Levi, and now at eBay, you have helped companies build super-inclusive teams; how can we become valued workplace team members from our first day on the job?

Work smart.
Focus on what drives impact and results.
Hint: It's the people who drive results.

Be you.
While you may need improvements
from time to time, your value will be highest
when you give people your most authentic self.

—CHARIS MARQUEZ
Vice President of Fashion at eBay
 LINKEDIN.COM/IN/CHARIS-MARQUEZ-7705632

What are your tips for producing the best videos for *Billboard*, and what is one piece of advice you wish you knew when you started?

"

My tips for producing the best *Billboard* videos would be to just have fun with it and create cool content. It's all about what the fans want . . . so asking artists unexpected questions that allow them to shine is always my technique. I love when fans get to see a different side of their favorite musician, whether it be their goofy side or even a moment of them being vulnerable. Celebs are just like us, so anytime they reveal something that allows their fans to relate to them on a deeper level is a total win!

Also, always just go with your gut when it comes to career moves and next steps. If you sink into being able to decipher what your heart truly desires, whether it be from a creative standpoint and how you want to express yourself through your work . . . or just a life standpoint, your gut will never lead you in the wrong direction.

And don't take yourself too seriously! Life is too short and it's supposed to be fun. So always go after what you truly want! It's never too late to start.

—CHELSEA BRIGGS
Host and Video Producer at Billboard
@CHELSEA_BRIGGS

40

> **What was it like to be the fourteenth employee at Snapchat, and what was it like when you pivoted to launch something new?**

My journey to Snapchat and now Yoni Circle was carved by being the most authentic version of myself. I wrote a story praising Snapchat while it was being largely criticized in the beginning, and when the story went viral, I got to know the team.

I was recruited to be their fourteenth employee and helped create and ultimately oversee the Our Story product, but this period of growth in my career halted when I was replaced by three older men. Listening to strangers' stories while sharing my own was essential to my healing process, so I knew it could help others, which led me to create Yoni Circle and sculpt my own authentic career path.

—CHLOË DRIMAL
Founder and CEO, Yoni Circle
CHAOTICKLOWY

41

You are a classically trained pianist, yet you have collaborated with some of the biggest names in pop and hip-hop . . . what's your advice for girls who want to learn to create new crossover styles in music?

"

Be authentic and don't be afraid of the word *no*. When you're starting a new sound, it's especially important for you to believe in it fully, so write and produce music that is authentic to you because that energy and passion will translate. So don't be afraid of hearing *no*. The entertainment industry doesn't like to take risks, so a new sound might scare some executives, but that doesn't mean it won't work. So keep going and keep asking for help along the way!

—CHLOE FLOWER
Pianist, Composer, and Music Producer
MISSCHLOEFLOWER

42

Your career has gone from flying U-2 spy planes to going to medical school and delivering babies; what is a piece of mentor advice you want us to remember when we are thinking about career paths and keeping things in perspective?

"

Don't say *no* to yourself.
It's never too late to pursue your passion.
As Billy Mills, American Indian Olympian, said:
Every passion has its destiny.
Embrace the struggle. Enjoy the level you're at.
Recognize that failures are inevitable.
Failure is a sign that your aim is not too low.

—CHOLENE ESPINOZA
US Air Force Pilot and OB/GYN Surgeon
LINKEDIN.COM/IN/CHOLENE-ESPINOZA-3B29784

43

What is the coolest thing about being a lawyer

for an organization as big as ViacomCBS, and

what would you tell girls considering career

paths in law right now?

One of the greatest things about my job is the breadth of
issues that I work on every single day . . . there is never
a dull moment, particularly in the entertainment industry!
Intellectual curiosity and the ability to be open-minded
and flexible are so critical for attorneys, particularly
given how quickly the landscape is evolving.

—CHRISTA D'ALIMONTE
Executive Vice President and General Counsel at ViacomCBS
LINKEDIN.COM/IN/CHRISTA-D-ALIMONTE-1775505

44

What are ways new candidates

can make profiles stand out

when applying for jobs?

What catches your eye most

when you look at résumés

of new graduates?

"

One commonality that we all share is that everyone faces challenges. What makes us unique is how we handle them and get to the other side. What I look for in a candidate is not the unblemished résumé where everything on paper shows a linear path forward. Life is most definitely not linear, and we learn our most potent lessons when trying to navigate uneven terrain or feeling around in the dark to turn on the light.

I'm looking for candidates who pivot to stay out front, no matter the size or scale of the challenge. If you're a recent graduate, you may not have a lengthy résumé, but how did you handle the pressure of a customer service job, what new idea did you suggest in an internship, what barriers did you overcome during this past year when humanity was put to the test? These are questions I ask in interviews, and they are questions that reveal true character.

My most profound lessons as a leader came from working in food services in my teens or lifeguarding and teaching swimming lessons. Don't underestimate how learning in any job can apply to a future career. And while it's tempting to portray someone who never trips or stumbles, that's not real life and certainly not the world of work. So show who you are and what you are capable of in the moments where you have been tested and flexed your resilience. Share how you dealt with defeat and conflicts because a little grit goes a long way.

—CHRISTY PAMBIANCHI
Executive Vice President and Chief People Officer at Intel
 LINKEDIN.COM/IN/CHRISTY-PAMBIANCHI

45

On your career journey, what inspired you

to become an advocate and catalyst for change,

and what are the steps to becoming a leader

for diversity and inclusion?

"

When I was a young girl I learned that using my voice mattered. After being consistently asked to stop being so loud, I finally learned how my voice could be powerful in advocating for others and bringing attention to subjects and people who need it. The most important step to becoming a leader is not being fearless but being fear-free. That was my mother's greatest lesson to me, to not let fear make decisions. Once you put fear aside you can start finding your voice and then using it for good.

—CLAUDIA ROMO EDELMAN
Mexican-Swiss Diplomat and Founder of
We Are All Human and Global GoalsCast
CLAUDIAROMOEDELMAN

When we are interviewing for first internships or jobs, what are the signs that a company truly values diversity, equality, and inclusion? How can we tell?

Many companies have developed a predictable formula for diversity, equity, and inclusion (DEI). At a minimum, you should look for a DEI lead; diversity recruitment, internship, training, and community programs; employee resource groups; and DEI transparency reports. That's good, but it's not enough.

You should also ask about the experience of underrepresented employees—beyond representation, which is important, ask about attrition and advancement rates for those employees. Look for signs of a company that is committed not just to bringing you in the door but also ensuring that you succeed.

—Daisy Auger-Domínguez
Chief People Officer at VICE Media Group
DAISYAUGERDOMINGUEZ

47

Why does running for student government in college matter, and what skills from your experience at MIT do you think transfer over to the work world?

66

Running for student government takes an
incredible amount of vulnerability and courage that
will set you up well for taking important risks in the
future. Student governments are constantly in need
of empathetic people who will prioritize student
engagement and equity while driving policy change.
As you give back to your community in public
service, you gain unparalleled experience leading
organizations and dealing with conflict resolution.

—DANIELLE GEATHERS
*First Black Woman Student Government
President at MIT*
@ DANIELLE.G_

As the youngest morning TV host in Chicago, were you underestimated because of your age or gender, and how did you handle that?

"

My most honest answer to this are words that I borrowed from Alicia Menendez. Her book *THE LIKEABILITY TRAP* changed my life. 'We know that when we enter a room, there are assumptions made about us, and many of us go to great lengths to undercut those assumptions. We know that we must always be prepared. We cannot afford to slip up. To us, 'Be yourself' can sound like a dare, a safe declaration only truly intended for those who are assumed to be competent, qualified, and powerful.' It can feel challenging and even exhausting to prove our competency—I've felt it often in my career. I don't think I've found a solution or an answer to it. But I do know that it's gotten easier to navigate as I've gotten older and gained more experience in my field. When you know yourself better and feel confident in what you bring to the table, the idea of having to prove yourself starts to wane. So, my best advice is to try to think less about others and focus more on yourself.

—DANIELLE ROBAY
TV Host and Journalist
DANIELLEROBAY

49

How did you arrive at your role at Space Tango, and how would you encourage girls to take on non-traditional career pathways in IT and STEM?

"

While working in the space industry was always on my vision board, Space Tango was not. The company actually didn't exist when I graduated high school, and now I'm a communications manager. I didn't foresee this path, and it would not have happened if I didn't lean into my passion for space. It's my passion that helped me push past my anxiety disorder to network with amazing women in the industry like Higher Orbits founder Michelle Lucas. Detours and hidden steps can lead us toward something better than we ever imagined.

—DANIELLE ROSALES
Communications Manager for Space Tango
 SPACEYUTE

50

You gave up law to make documentaries with legends like John Lewis and Oprah, and you did it without going to film school; what is your advice to girls about changing careers to chase their dreams?

"

Listen to that quiet but persistent voice in your head asking 'what if?' What if I quit this job and moved? What if I told my boss I want to try something new? What if I didn't question myself? Becoming a film director was never in my plans. And yet it's the perfect job for me. I couldn't know that when I was 18 or even 25. I had to keep listening to my gut about each next career step. Each job brought me closer to my dream job and now I can't imagine doing anything else. Except maybe making furniture.

What if?

—DAWN PORTER
Award-Winning Film Director, Trilogy Films
 DAWNPORTER

51

Why are early female role models so important in STEM?

"

Role models, specifically female role models, in media are so badly needed—and this is why:

Before high school I would have pictured an engineer as some nerdy guy with no friends. If I had known that I could love math, study engineering, and wind up as the CEO of a toy company and now a media organization, I would have been even better prepared for my classes in college and the opportunities that came after. My world would have changed sooner.

—DEBBIE STERLING
Founder and CEO of GoldieBlox
DEBSTERLING

52

How would you advise young classical musicians who ultimately want to move into leadership roles like managing an orchestra?

"

It is sometimes a challenge to get that first job, but finding a position at a major musical institution, even at the entry level, allows you to gain an overview of the many different facets of orchestra and music management.

From there you can not only broaden your management knowledge base, but potentially gain experience in areas unfamiliar to you.

—DEBORAH BORDA
President and CEO of the New York Philharmonic
@NYPHILHARMONIC

53

When starting out, people usually advise us to start at the bottom. Do you agree? Did you? How long should we expect to wait to advance to our dream jobs?

> "

I started at 'the bottom' . . . earned a great promotion, and then suddenly, unexpectedly found myself at the bottom again. It was frustrating and demoralizing, but it did teach me early on that you have to take ownership of your career. I pushed for more opportunities. At the time, I said something not quite as eloquent as this: *'Sure I'll continue to do this job that you know that I can do, since I've excelled at it for two years, but I also need to grow, so if I am willing to do more to advance my career, I need you to help me do that.'* It was a really tough pill to swallow at the time. But looking back, no one cares that I was a PA for two years or four years. I was working at the top morning show in television, building on experience that I could not get anywhere else.

My dream job? I'm still waiting. My dream job has changed over the course of my career. If I am being honest, sometimes I have just dreamed about getting a job. For me, it has become more important to love what I do. I may not love my job every day—after all, they still have to pay me to do it. But I love the work. I love the creative process. I love the result.

Other wisdom? Find *your* work-life balance. Your life will have highs and lows—many of which you cannot predict or change. Some of them will be personal; some will be professional. Define your boundaries, and know that over the course of your career, those goal posts will change. They should. Work does not equal life. Life does not equal work. There are times in your life when your career will be the most important thing in your life. *That is OK.* At other times your family and personal life will take precedence. *That is OK.* Your best friend will get married the weekend before a big project at work is due. *Go to the wedding.* Also, *get the project done.* But also know that you will have to choose between work and life many times throughout your career, and there will always be sacrifice. Just make sure that it is on your terms.

—DEE DEE THOMAS
Senior Director/Senior EP, Live Content at Yahoo Finance Live
 LINKEDIN.COM/IN/DEEDEETHOMAS

54

What is your advice to aspiring authors ready to pitch their first book to an agent— what makes a great pitch and what's one common mistake to avoid?

Show in your proposal what your proposed book would be like versus *tell*. The writing itself in the proposal matters just as much as the idea. Answer the question: Why am I the perfect person to bring this particular book to the world? Make that case.

—Diana Kapp
Author of GIRLS WHO RUN THE WORLD
and GIRLS WHO GREEN THE WORLD
@GIRLSWHOBOOKS

There are probably a lot of people who expected you to go into fashion and design given your art background; where did you find the courage to do the unexpected and start a candy empire?

" "

I'm happy that I've been able to create a lifestyle brand and *retail-tainment* experience that merges fashion, art, and pop culture with candy. I have enjoyed designing delicious edible products as well as candy-shaped and color-inspired items from beauty products, handbags, toys, and apparel to dinnerware, stationery, and beyond! My ambition and faith in being an entrepreneur continue to grow with the support and grounding influence of my close family and lifelong friends. Their infectious positivity, mentorship, and encouragement of me to follow my gut has been instrumental in how I have followed my dreams and developed Dylan's Candy Bar.

—DYLAN LAUREN
CEO of Dylan's Candy Bar
 DYLANSCANDYBAR

56

We are coming of age watching and listening to the MAKERS stories you tell; what are a few traits or skill sets that make a MAKER?

"

MAKERS come in all shapes and sizes because there is no one way to lead or one accomplishment bigger than the other. But I found that behind every MAKER is a purpose-driven woman with an ability to block out the naysayers or move beyond failure to reach her goal.

—Dyllan McGee
Founder and Executive Producer of MAKERS Women
MAKERSWOMEN

57

What inspired you to pursue the field of breast cancer surgery and research, and how do you know when it's time to stay in a position and be patient, or push to make the next step in your career?

"

I never thought I would be a surgeon; however, when I spent time with surgeons during medical school I fell in love with it. I am a visual learner, very good with my hands, and love seeing immediate results. I always wanted to care for patients with cancer, to help people during their most vulnerable times. I have learned from my patients about the strength of the human spirit and resilience.

Asking research questions, collecting data, and sharing your results with others helps progress treatment options for patients. When you feel like you are not learning anymore, then it is time for the next step in your career to continue to grow.

—ELENI ANASTASIA TOUSIMIS
Director, Scully-Welsh Cleveland Clinic Cancer Center
 LINKEDIN.COM/IN/ELENI-ANASTASIA-TOUSIMIS-99602479

What is it like to drive social media for a company like Lilly Pulitzer, and how do you decide on each new campaign?

"

Driving social media for a company like Lilly Pulitzer is an honor, an inspiration, and a challenge (in the best way possible). Campaign ideas often form from my favorite kind of brainstorms—where one thought-starter kicks off, more spark from there, and then it builds to something bigger and stronger than one person could have dreamed alone. We're also often inspired by our own community, and of course, by Lilly.

—ELENI MCCREADY
Senior Director of Social Media, Promotions,
Brand Marketing, and Community at Lilly Pulitzer
 LINKEDIN.COM/IN/ELENIMCCREADY

59

What do our social media profiles say about us as candidates when companies are looking to hire, and do you pay attention to similar things when helping big companies like McDonald's drive social marketing campaigns?

"

Creating and refining your personal brand is critical to succeeding in the business world, and our social media profiles are a big part of that. So it's important to keep your social media channels up to date and appropriate to your specific field, while also giving followers a peek at who you really are, not just as an employee, but as a person.

This is true for companies as well—part of my responsibilities are leading the team that amplifies McDonald's voice through our social media content strategy and making sure we stay relevant to our customers, all the while allowing our brand personality to shine through. And we get to poke fun at ourselves every now and then . . . like real people.

—ELIZABETH CAMPBELL
Senior Director of Marketing and Cultural
Engagement Strategy at McDonald's
 LINKEDIN.COM/IN/ELIZABETHACAMPBELL1

60

When facing obstacles or unexpected challenges at work, what is one thing you want girls to keep in mind to keep anxiety at bay?

"

Obstacles and challenges are part of life, and often the only part we can control is our reaction to them. First, and this can be really hard, do not take setbacks personally. They are learning experiences if you let them be so. Always remember, whatever is happening to you now has happened to someone else before you. Reach out to someone you trust—people want to help, and will, if you ask them.

Anxiety thrives in isolation. If you keep it a secret, it will grow. Sometimes just telling someone you feel anxious or overwhelmed is all you need for relief. And the true gift is when that someone guides you, or shares their own perspective on how they dealt with setbacks or insecurity. Finally, don't forget to pay it forward. Encourage and support the women who you see struggle to find their footing in what can be an unforgiving world.

—ELIZABETH VARGAS
TV Journalist and Author
🐦 EVARGASTV

61

What advice would you give us about setting up smart habits as we take our first steps in the work world?

"

Be the person who listens the most in a room;
when it's your time to share you'll be well informed!

—Emme
Model, Author, and TV Personality
 THEOFFICIALEMME

How did decades in the US military build your leadership and mentoring skills, and when have you felt the most brave?

"

My thirty-two-plus years of military service helped me truly understand that knowledge is not enough and average is not a place to stay for long. Leadership is not a title, position, or rank; it is an amazing skill we can learn to become significant in someone's life. Leadership is influence, sacrifice, love, expertise, credibility, and being humble. When I felt the most brave was when I was able to defend and protect the ones who counted on me to be their voice.

—ERICKA KELLY
US Veteran, Speaker, and Leadership Expert
 LINKEDIN.COM/IN/ERICKA-KELLY-ENTERPRISES

63

Why are the strategies learned at the poker table vital for women at the boardroom table?

"

The lessons learned at the poker table apply to
every table, from the classroom to the boardroom
table. Going all-in gives you the confidence to take a
risk and ask for a promotion; raising the stakes helps
you negotiate better; and practicing concentration,
resilience, computation, and probability skills
help you make strategic decisions with imperfect
information. And the most important lesson—which
is especially important for young women to learn
—is that if you don't sit at the table, you can't play,
and if you don't play, you can't ever win.

—ERIN LYDON
Managing Director at Poker Power
in LINKEDIN.COM/IN/ERIN-LYDON-MBA

We *love* that you are making career advice about the film industry so accessible on TikTok! What are a few insider tips you can share with aspiring filmmakers here?

66

For anyone who wants to work in the film
industry, just know that:

1. There are no rules.

2. No one knows what they're doing.

3. Be flexible and adapt to change.
A director/production company that's really hot
this year might be old news next year.

4. Follow your gut.

5. You belong just as much as anyone else.

6. Story is king in this industry. There will always
be those with more connections and more money
. . . but at the end of the day, story trumps all.

—ERIN McGOFF
*Director and Editor, TikTok Content Creator,
and Documentary Filmmaker*
♪ ERINMCGOFF

65

What are ways that we

can build careers in philanthropy;

in other words, how can wanting to give back

become a career path for the future?

"

First and foremost, identify how you'd like to give back
and what types of giving activities you enjoy doing. Once you've
identified those two things, you can then begin volunteering
with, interning with, and applying for entry-level positions
with non-profits that align with your goals.

—Etoy Ridgnal
Global Head of Strategy and Partnerships,
The Will & Jada Smith Family Foundation
@ETOYRIDGNAL

66

What makes brand-new LinkedIn profiles stand

out, and how can those entering

the work world for the first time leverage all

that LinkedIn has to offer?

"

What makes a brand-new LinkedIn profile stand out? *Authenticity!*
Your profile is your story, and that will set you apart from others.
Make your unique personality come to life through
your photo, background image, and summary.

How can you leverage all that LinkedIn has to offer? *The key is
your network.* Don't be shy to send a connection request with a short
personal note to people who have a job or work at a company you
find interesting. By connecting with others you will get insights and
inspiration, and new opportunities will open up for you in no time.
Take the first step and connect with me!

—GABY WASENSTEINER
Brand Marketing Manager at LinkedIn
LINKEDIN.COM/IN/WASENSTEINER/

67

What is the key to writing unforgettable thank-you notes, and how can this skill be used well in the workplace?

"

The key to writing unforgettable thank-you notes is to write from the heart. I spent a month thanking 30 career mentors, and in those notes I recalled the ways they made a difference—advice they gave, introductions they made, examples they modeled—and explained the long-term impact on my career path.

Expressing gratitude, I learned, is the most authentic way to network. The notes I sent out led to catch-up lunches and conversations, and one former boss even convinced me to write a book about my year sending 365 thank-you notes.

—GINA HAMADEY
Author of I WANT TO THANK YOU and
Founder of Penknife Media
GINA.HAMADEY

68

How do students go about paying for professional schools without going into a crazy amount of debt?

"

Simply asking this question shows you're planning ahead—and that's your first step. Explore options to lower the cost: check if your employer will cover or reimburse your tuition, research and apply for scholarships and grants, or work as a teaching assistant (TA) if your university will lower the tuition you owe in return. You can also consider going to school part-time so you can maintain your income while you work toward your advanced degree.

—GISELLE RIVERA
Head of Rising Generation Segment at UBS
LINKEDIN.COM/IN/GISELLEMRIVERA

What makes a great cover letter
when new graduates apply for jobs
at NBC (do we even need them?),
and what kind of résumés stand
out the most to you?

"

Cover letters are not necessary unless it's specifically requested or you are trying to explain something such as a change in career. Most hiring managers and recruiters look through hundreds of résumés for each open role, so there is not a lot of time to read them. For your résumé to stand out, it's important to get the hiring manager's attention by ensuring it's organized and concise. You should use key buzzwords that are relevant and customized to the opportunity you are seeking. It's not enough to list out your job description; you should also demonstrate *how you made an impact in your role*. Quantify your contributions and include metrics to help convey how effective you were in your role. Résumés can reflect your personal style. Make sure colors, graphics, and fonts are used to enhance and not distract the reader from your accomplishments. Try to keep your résumé to one page and don't forget to double-check your spelling and grammar!

—GIULIANA EMINENTE RAMSARRAN
Vice President, Human Resources at NBCUniversal Media
LINKEDIN.COM/IN/GIULIANA-EMINENTE-RAMSARRAN-4A898A4

70

We heard that you launched Thousand on Kickstarter in an effort to save 1,000 lives; what advice would you give entrepreneurial girls who have startups in mind that could someday make a difference in their communities?

"

There are lots of people who want to be their own boss,
or run a company, but there are far fewer who want to
use the power of business to help their community
and the planet. So the most important thing you can
do is to go for it! The world needs more people like
you to show up and have a voice.

—GLORIA HWANG
Founder and CEO of Thousand
EXPLORETHOUSAND

We've heard you say that
you didn't leave your dream job
to launch The Laundress, but that you
"graduated" from it; how can we tell
when it's time to leave a dream job,
and what did you say to those who
tried to discourage you?

"

I *loved* my job! I loved my co-workers, my boss, my company, I loved it all! But there is also a time when you need to move on. For instance, you loved summer camp but it was time to grow up and get a job or a summer experience to prepare you for college, or you loved high school but it was time to move on to college and have the next more advanced and enriching academic and social experiences; leaving my job was very similar to that. I had so many amazing work experiences and opportunities in such a short amount of time, all while I spent two years building the foundation to launch my company. I had a launch date goal, I had hired and trained my assistant to be the replacement for me for over a year, and I had my departure date set for six months after I launched the brand (all with my boss's support!). I *was* ready to graduate! While my friends seemed to be excited about the adventure, my family was not. I was confident with my plans, my business idea, and my willingness to give every ounce in me to succeed.

—GWEN WHITING
Founder of The Laundress
GWENLWHITING

72

What would you say to girls eager to pursue graduate degrees but who might be apprehensive (or discouraged by others) because they have a disability? What kept you focused when you entered Harvard Law School?

"

I encountered numerous challenges as the first Deafblind person in so many spaces. It was both exhausting and rewarding. Each time you remove a barrier, you clear the path for the next person who comes after you. For me, knowing that the process of dismantling obstacles benefits the entire community is energizing.

—HABEN GIRMA
Human Rights Lawyer and Author of HABEN: THE DEAFBLIND WOMAN WHO CONQUERED HARVARD LAW
HABENGIRMA

How did you stay resilient and persistent in the face of obstacles in your life and career (even when people wanted you to change the spelling of your name), and what is one thing you want girls entering the workforce to know about those traits?

66

The key to being successful in the workplace is to surround yourself only with positive people. I love the quote, 'You are the average of the five people you spend the most time with.' This is true in the workplace too. Choose wisely . . . Don't hang around the gossips, or the negative people; find the people who are kind. And do not listen to anyone who says you can't be both nice and successful. It's not true. You can be deeply kind and wildly successful. The other important factor is to never quit. It sounds basic, but there is an open road ahead. So many people will drop out, as they cannot handle the long hours, the difficult assignments, and moving from city to city. If you just hang in there, you will find your long runway awaits.

—HODA KOTB
Co-Anchor, TODAY and Co-Host of
TODAY with Hoda & Jenna
HODAKOTB

74

How did you score an internship at Xbox, and what is one piece of advice you would give to other girls about making the most out of their internships?

"

My motto is 'opportunities compound.' This simple yet powerful idea led to earning an internship at Xbox, a childhood dream of mine. Each course completed, project built, challenge overcome, volunteering opportunity taken, and internship landed built on top of one other and led to new, exciting opportunities to push my career toward my ultimate goal.

For those looking to maximize your internships and career at large, seek out opportunities to emphasize your strengths, say *yes* to challenges that scare you, and pay it forward to those following in your footsteps. Together these combine to accelerate your progression, emphasize a growth mindset, and improve the industry at large whilst also building you a strategic network.

—HOLLY BOOTHROYD
Xbox Intern Turned Microsoft Software Engineer
HERHELLOWORLD

75

Did it ever bother you to be the only female surgeon in the operating room?

"

Most of the time I am the only woman surgeon in the operating room. I never really thought about this until you asked me the question. On the other hand, I'll share with you an episode where I realized I was 'the only woman.' During my fellowship, my scientific neurosurgery work was accepted for a platform presentation at our national meeting. The title of my presentation was announced, followed by: *This work will be presented by Dr. I. M. Germano.* As I was walking on the podium, the presenter rapidly corrected himself: 'I am sorry, Dr. Germano could not attend the meeting and has sent his nurse.' I stood up in front of the microphone, I looked around the huge auditorium, and I saw myself on multiple large screens. I wanted to run away.

Instead I said: 'I *am* Dr. Isabelle M. Germano.
I am here to present my neurosurgery work.'

—ISABELLE M. GERMANO
Neurosurgeon
in LINKEDIN.COM/IN/ISABELLE-GERMANO-1A5A08108

What were the first steps you took to get your art seen in a gallery setting, and what advice would you give to those of us nervous to show our art publicly for the first time?

"

Presentation is key—I would recommend only sharing high-quality and well-lit images of your artwork. Find a friend who is a photographer and ask for a good price or consider a trade. See as much work in galleries, artist-run spaces, and museums as you possibly can. Imagine your pieces in the spaces you visit, as this will help dispel any nerves you have about whether your work is ready for public exhibition.

—ISCA GREENFIELD-SANDERS
Painter
ⓞ ISCAGS

77

As Walmart's first-ever Chief Customer Officer, what is the best piece of mentor advice you ever received, and what is your advice to anyone who will be "the first" in her particular role?

"

A boss once told me to 'Take the hard job. The job no one wants.' For whatever reason, you may be asked to tackle a role or job that isn't the most glamorous. I'm here to tell you to take the job and do the best work you can in the role. Use the opportunity to learn and to dissect, process, and feed your curiosity. It will help you become a well-rounded professional.

This philosophy led me to my dream role—Walmart's first Chief Customer Officer—where I listen to customers, serve as their advocate, and help solve their problems in a way only Walmart can. My path leading this organization was born from a myriad of earlier roles that I may have been less excited about but made me the fit for my dream role. Each of you has the distinct ability to put an indelible mark on any role or task in your career.

—JANEY WHITESIDE
Chief Customer Officer of Walmart
 JANEYWHITESIDE

78

What are three things
we should do with our first
paychecks to establish smart
money habits?

“

1. Look at it. It's pretty common to get paid for the first time and think, *Holy moly, where did all my money go?* You've just discovered the difference between your gross income (before taxes) and your net income (after taxes are taken out). The federal and some state governments take some; so does Social Security and Medicare (that's the line called FICA; you'll get it back in healthcare and a pension when you're older). The important thing? You must, must, *must* live on your net income, not your gross income.

2. Save before you spend. When we're talking about money habits, this is the most important of all. Every single time you get paid, some money—aim for 15 percent, more if possible—should come right out of your check and go into savings and investments. If you have a retirement plan at work, this may happen automatically. If not, you want to set it up so that the money moves automatically—out of your checking account and into savings—every time a paycheck gets deposited. Why automatically? So that you don't have to think about it every time.

3. Put those savings to work. Money saved in a bank account is nice. It can help you get through an emergency or pay for a vacation. But money you put into investments—like stocks and mutual funds—can help you build long-lasting wealth. Although you want to have enough cash in the bank to get you through an emergency (a few thousand to start, eventually building to three to six months' worth), make sure that you are also investing some of those savings. They need to be working for you as hard as you're working for yourself.

—JEAN CHATZKY
CEO and Founder of HerMoney Media, Former Financial Editor of the TODAY Show, and Author of WOMEN WITH MONEY
 JEANCHATZKY

79

> What advice would you give to young women getting ready to present their first business pitch to potential investors, especially if we are pitching on TV?

Do your homework! Preparation means everything. Make sure you know about the people you are pitching to, their business, their source of capital, their priorities, their background (professional history, academic credentials, location, etc.), then make sure your pitch is tailored to their needs!

—Jeannine Shao Collins
President of SEEHER and Cofounder/CEO of Girl Starter
in LINKEDIN.COM/IN/JEANNINE-SHAO-COLLINS-54A4A58

What are careers at the intersection of finance and tech that you think new graduates should be watching, and what is one piece of mentor advice you want us to remember?

"

I encourage all new graduates—particularly young women—looking to get into finance and tech careers to not be defined by one industry or market. Focus on roles that use fintech to help companies find a better way of doing things, and you'll vastly expand your job opportunities. And when you land the job and find yourself in your first few meetings, remember to speak up. Your opinions, ideas, and analysis are unique and add value to the conversation. If you want to run that same meeting one day, people need to hear from you now.

—JENNIFER JUST
Cofounder, PEAK6 Investments
in LINKEDIN.COM/IN/JENNIFER-JUST-46208A11

81

What would you tell girls about being underestimated in the workplace (how to handle that) and about underestimating ourselves (how to avoid *that*)?

My advice about underestimating ourselves is to stop—
we can do anything boys can do in business and they don't
have the power over your mind—only you do.

My advice to girls about being underestimated in the
workplace is to call it out. Staying silent is no longer an
option if we want change. Find your allies in the workplace
and have them support you in calling it out as well.

—JENNIFER JUSTICE
*CEO and Founder, The Justice Dept and Host of Takin'
Care of Lady Business Podcast*
 THEJUSTICE.DEPT

Are there jobs that don't exist now that you think will be needed later with the advancement in space travel... and if so, what skills will we need to do them really well?

66

Yes! NASA is moving closer and closer to a commercial model for low Earth orbit activities. With private astronaut missions, development of new space stations, and the emergence of space commerce, girls and women of color will need to have a diversified education. STEM will always be key, but a person with a 'STEAM' background and solid business skills will be in a prime position for success in the space industry.

— JENNIFER SCOTT WILLIAMS
Manager, Applications Client Support Branch,
International Space Station Research Integration Office
NASA Johnson Space Center
 LINKEDIN.COM/IN/JENNIFER-SCOTT-WILLIAMS-NASA

83

How do you handle nerves before big auditions, and do you have any tips for girls preparing for their own first big auditions or job interviews?

"

My favorite acting teacher told me over and over the audition room was a sandbox. If I prepared, all I had to do was go in and kick up sand. It gave me a ton of confidence and freedom and taught me to have fun with auditions instead of dreading them.

—JILLIAN DAVIS

Actress

 JILLIEDAVIS

84

You were a fashion major who joined NBC as part of the Page Program and wound up winning multiple Emmys and a Gracie Award. How did you stand out in your early career roles, and what advice do you have for girls who want to distinguish themselves in their first industry jobs?

Two words—work ethic. I learned early on that if I wanted to stand out, I was going to get the job done. I didn't go to an Ivy League university. I had internships, but not with any major networks or well-known shows, and I didn't have any connections. All I had was my hunger to succeed. If I wanted to stand out, I was going to have to work for it, and I did. I took on as many assignments as I could, and I never let them see me sweat. After all, there were countless people who would take my job in a hot second, and I wanted to outshine them all.

—JOANNE LaMARCA MATHISEN
Former Executive Producer at NBC
 LINKEDIN.COM/IN/JOANNE-LAMARCA-MATHISEN-26352264

What makes an amazing intern,

and what skills or traits do you look for

when considering whether to hire

an intern for a full-time position?

"

Interns who possess a high level of self-awareness, personal drive, and resourcefulness have been the most successful in my experience. A willingness to proactively reach out, form relationships, and speak up have been some of the traits that have transitioned many of our interns into full-time hires. It's OK not to know everything! Ask questions, speak up, and show your curiosity and passion every chance you can.

—JOLENE DELISLE
Founder of The Working Assembly
 WORKINGASSEMBLY

86

How can girls interested in tech careers start to build their networks early, and how has your network helped you lead at places like Apple, AmEx, and Tile?

"

I highly encourage girls interested in tech careers to start joining some of the amazing women in tech communities that exist as a way to network with others. Check out elpha.com, Girls Who Code, and Women Who Code, just to name a few. Networking has been invaluable for me—most of the roles I've had in my career I learned about through a connection. Sometimes we are afraid to reach out and start a conversation, but I encourage you to be brave! Each and every one of us has different backgrounds and experiences, and when we share from that place of vulnerability, you will find people want to engage with you.

—JOSSIE HAINES
Vice President of Software Engineering and Head of DEI at Tile
 LINKEDIN.COM/IN/JOSSIEMANN

87

What are three things that
girls might not know about careers in
construction trades like plumbing, carpentry,
and electrical, and what is your advice to
girls eyeing male-dominated
fields in general?

"

Three things girls might not know about careers
in construction are: One, they are very lucrative and
the skills you learn will ensure you always have a job.
Two, plumbers do so much more than installing toilets:
for example, they oversee the all-important gas lines in
hospitals that help doctors perform surgeries. Three,
the cloud data storage servers are built and
maintained by electricians.

My advice to girls eyeing a career in male-dominated
fields is just do it; remember that jobs don't
have genders and be a rebel girl.

—JUDALINE CASSIDY
Plumber, Speaker, and CVO of Tools and Tiaras, Inc.
JUDALINE6

We love that Girl Scouts everywhere have a network for life—what are some smart ways Girl Scouts can leverage this community and connect with other alums as they enter the workforce?

"

Girl Scouts is perhaps the first network a girl has access to in her journey to adulthood. From the sisterhood of her troopmates to countless supportive adults in her community, she's able to foster important connections with other women to help with her career and life journey. I've heard of so many smart ways women have leveraged their Girl Scout connections—like reaching out to their local council to inquire about job opportunities, or including Girl Scouts on their résumé, and convening monthly Girl Scout alum luncheons at their place of work.

Learn more about becoming part of the official Girl Scout Network for alums and supporters at www.girlscouts.org/ girlscoutnetwork, where you can attend virtual Campfire Chats, explore ways to volunteer, receive news about innovative alums, and so much more.

—Judith Batty
CEO of Girl Scouts of the USA
 GIRLSCOUTS

"

What have you learned about the

art of feedback (giving it or getting it)

that you think everyone should know before

their first performance reviews?

"

Go into receiving feedback with a positive mindset. Know that any
constructive criticism is intended to make you stronger! Success comes
when you are open to listening and constantly evolving to be
the best possible version of yourself.

—JULIE DAVIS
Vice President, Private Wealth Management at Goldman Sachs
in LINKEDIN.COM/IN/JULIEJDAVIS

How can girls with strong STEM skills get noticed by companies like Nike? Also, what STEM classes, majors, or early internships are helpful when eyeing a career with Nike?

"

In our current environment, data analytics, engineering of all types, and business intelligence strategy are premiere areas of interest. That said, dive deep into a craft or calling that makes your heart rate quicken and refine how that which makes your heart zing can often make a company's best even better. Résumés and one-pagers can denote your experience, but demonstrating servant leadership, diversity of thought, and bold innovation early in your career will not only add to your skill set but will make you, your teammates, and your world better in the long run.

—JULIE LANGFORD
Director, Nike North America Technical Product Management,
Marketing Tech
 LINKEDIN.COM/IN/JULIELANGFORD

91

How did you find the courage to
go from one small idea to an empire?
In other words, how did you first
become "undaunted"?

"

There are endless reasons why new beverage companies fail, but when a Coke exec dismissed my idea for an unsweetened flavored water, I realized that I could build a new category that was focused on helping people get healthy. The big guys were so focused on sweet drinks that they couldn't imagine selling an unsweetened flavored water. There was a window of time where I could build it. *I had to do it.* It was my mission. It was my purpose.

—KARA GOLDIN
Founder and CEO of Hint, Inc. and
Author of UNDAUNTED
@KARAGOLDIN

What is your advice to girls
who know they want to be surgeons
but worry about being told
no because of a physical disability?

"

My dad once told me that we always have three sides.
There is the side we see when we think of ourselves, the side
others see when they think of us, and finally, reality.

As a woman wearing a full-length leg brace in the 1980s, wanting
to be a neurosurgeon seemed a tall order. I had received an excellent
education and was coming to the end of my medical education, yet there
were assumptions made every day about 'what would be best' for me. But I
knew what I loved and I knew what inspired me. I loved neurosurgery and
have never regretted setting out on an uncharted course. In some
ways, not having to follow someone else's path but
creating my own has been liberating.

Mentors can help guide, but in the end the decisions we make must come
from within. To that end, it is important to test one's dreams to see if they
are feasible . . . assess the reality of your individual goals. But never lose sight
of your dreams and don't be afraid to question the perceptions of others.

Choosing to be a neurosurgeon may not have been what others
would have chosen for me but in the end it has been a rewarding and exciting
career that I have never regretted undertaking.
Dare to think big and create your own path!

—KARIN MURASZKO
*Chair of Neurosurgery at the University of Michigan and the First Woman
to Head a Neurosurgery Department at a Medical School in the US*
 LINKEDIN.COM/IN/KARIN-MURASZKO-MD-FACS-B7422849

> *How can hobbies like 3D printing help address a global pandemic, and what future uses of 3D printing do you see that STEM girls should know about?*

"

3D printing is what enabled me to donate 82,000 pieces of personal protective equipment during a pandemic. In the future, girls in STEM will be able to 3D print organs to help people who need transplants and so much more. My 3D printer makes me feel like the world is my oyster. Also, remember that STEM is everywhere, and engineers belong in all career areas—from creative to fashion to art!

—Karina Popovich
Founder of Makers for Change
🅞 KARINA.POPOVICH

94

Your photographs have started global movements and make girls everywhere feel more confident; what classes or jobs do you think best prepared you for a career in photography?

"

I always wanted to work in a visual medium. I started with internships at Nickelodeon and *GERALDO* (yes, *that* Geraldo!). One of my first jobs out of college was as an editor at CNN, and I then moved to work at an ad agency producing commercials. I am very thankful that I had a whole career making things look compelling on screen and then took that knowledge into my photography.

—KATE T. PARKER
Photographer, Creator of the STRONG IS THE NEW PRETTY Series, and New York Times Bestselling Author
KATETPARKER

95

What is your best overall advice for young women starting out?

"

The single most important advice I'd give to anyone, especially young women, is to never allow 'the world' to define them. Instead let the One who created the world and created them in His image define who they are and how precious and valuable they are as unique individuals.

—KATHIE LEE GIFFORD
TV Host, Singer, Songwriter, Actor, and Author
 KATHIELGIFFORD

96

How can we avoid making big money mistakes, and what are the finance topics we should be talking about right now?

1. The longer the time period you have to grow your money, the better. So the sooner you start investing, the longer it has time to compound. Compound just means your money makes money and this becomes a snowball effect, which gets larger and larger.

2. Have a budget. Know how much you spend every week or every month, which expenses are recurring, and which ones are not.

3. Know that money is a tool, and it is OK to talk about money and communicate your goals and priorities with your friends or family.

—KATHLEEN ENTWISTLE
Top Forbes Advisor
in LINKEDIN.COM/IN/KATHLEENENTWISTLE

What did it feel like to direct and produce your first award-winning film, and what skills are most helpful for girls looking to enter the filmmaking field?

" "

Making *FLY LIKE A GIRL* was an emotional roller coaster. It was exhilarating, fulfilling, surreal, humbling, and terrifying all at once. It was one of the most incredible experiences, and I am so grateful for every moment.

From the technical language to the creative process, filmmaking can be intimidating in many ways. Seek out groups that support emerging filmmakers. Don't be afraid to ask questions and be willing to keep learning.

—KATIE MCENTIRE WIATT
Director and Coeditor of FLY LIKE A GIRL
 KMWIATT

98

What do you want girls getting ready for careers in sports to remember?

"

Anybody who knows me knows that I have spent countless hours advocating for young girls, advocating for young women and really trying to help them advance their careers. That's something that is so important to me. Now having this high-profile position, where you're out in public more . . . There is an adage: 'You can't be it if you can't see it.' I guess I would suggest to them, *now you can see it.* And so I look forward to hearing their stories and how inspired they are to pursue a job in sports—a job in baseball—and to reach for the stars.

—KIM NG
Miami Marlins General Manager*
 MARLINS

*Provided by Kim Ng after her press conference on November 16, 2020

99

What does it feel like to have created a piece of art that will inspire girls our age for so many generations, and what is one piece of advice you would give to fearless artists who also want to impact the world?

"

The fact that I could use realism as a tool to send a clear social message was breathtaking! This is something that cannot be done with distorted or abstract art, and the realization gave me a new appreciation for realism. Stimulating change through uplifting all who emulate the *Fearless Girl* pose is to fully participate in society as an active, passionate, and caring member, and *that* feels fabulous!

Always begin by asking the question, 'What am I trying to *say*, and *what* is the best way to convey it? What audience am I speaking to, and how can I ensure they understand the message?' These questions become the problem you must solve. Remember to speak to what is most familiar and use your passion to give the work impact!

—KRISTEN VISBAL
Creator of the Fearless Girl Statue
VISBALSCULPTURE

100

> # What are three things we should know about what makes a great presentation? Whether internally or to clients, what should we know before we start?

A presentation tells a story through messaging and visuals; the content should guide the presentation and conversation but should not serve as reading material for the audience. Begin with drafting the story, or what is considered the talk track, and then build the presentation to support the story. Less is more; you, as the presenter, should be the focal point of the presentation. It is important to engage with the audience and allow the presentation to serve as the visual device that supports you as the main act in the show.

—Laura Smith
Senior Vice President at Racepoint Global
LINKEDIN.COM/IN/LAURAMCCARTHYSMITH

101

Given that women head only 3 percent

of the world's top one hundred airlines, what is

your advice to girls eyeing careers

in highly male-dominated fields?

My biggest advice is to never overcompensate
for being a woman. What I find to be the most impactful is
approaching any situation with facts and presenting in a
low and steady voice—this displays confidence
without overcompensation.

—LEONA QI
President of VistaJet
LINKEDIN.COM/IN/LEONA-QI-2689642

102

What is the best way to follow up after an interview?
Should we email, send an actual note, call?
What's the best way to leave a good impression

after we walk out the door?

"

The best way to follow up after an interview is to send a personalized thank-you email within two days of your interview. Make sure your note is personal and refers to something specific from your conversation. Follow up, timing, and tone are key. Senior leaders are busy—if you wait too long, they will forget about you. Follow up within two days, and say something that jogs their memory.

—LILIANA PETROVA
CEO of The Petrova Experience
THEPETROVAEXPERIENCE

103

What do you want today's girls to know about salary negotiation before they enter the workforce?

"

My advice for girls about salary negotiation is to have confidence and courage to have a conversation about salary. Confidence is knowing what value you would provide for the job and courage will provide the voice to sell your value.

Your starting salary is very important—if you start too low you can *never* catch up! Lost salary is gone forever!

—LILLY LEDBETTER
Equal Pay Advocate and Inspiration for
the Lilly Ledbetter Fair Pay Act
🐦 LILLY_LEDBETTER

104

"

How did you know that your cofounder was the right person, and what do you want us to know about joining forces with others to build big ideas?

"

Picking a business partner is like choosing a life partner because it's basically a marriage. I knew Serena was the right partner for Serena & Lily for five primary reasons:

1. Chemistry is paramount

2. Shared character values

3. Shared vision of what we wanted to bring into the world

4. Mutual respect over different domain ownership

5. Ability to have transparent communications

—LILY KANTER

Cofounder of Serena & Lily

LINKEDIN.COM/IN/LILY-KANTER-6805771

105

Was there ever a time when a mentor gave you game-changing advice that moved your career in a different (or unexpected) direction? If *yes*, were you hesitant about taking the advice?

Several years ago, I secured my first executive-level job with my dream company. But it required a cross-country move, which I wasn't eager to do. A mentor enthusiastically encouraged me to accept the role and move. His reasoning was that I wouldn't be in that job forever, and if I didn't like the new town, I could always move back. He said, 'No one is going to pull up the drawbridge.' I went for it. The increase in job title and compensation has been life-changing, and I was able to move back home just a few years later.

—LINDA CROWE
Community Program Director at IBM
LLCROWE

106

"

Why are all-female networks like Chief so
important for women in the most senior roles . . .
and how can girls starting first jobs build
their own strong networks?

"

Networks like Chief unite and support women leaders so they can
effect change from the top down, creating ripple effects within
their organizations that will result in progressive change. Women
early in their careers should begin building their own networks by
forging connections outside of their domain expertise and pursuing
diverse relationships over short-term transactions.

—LINDSAY KAPLAN
Cofounder of Chief
LINDSAYKAP

107

What is a typical day at Google like for you, and what is one amazing thing about working at Google that most people don't know?

66

A typical day at Google is fast-paced, filled to the brim with new learnings and strategic conversations with partners about their business goals and new opportunities to drive success. What I love most about Google that you would only know if you worked there are the people.

Google prides itself on not just hiring smart individuals, but people who are well rounded and want to thrive in a growing environment. Nineteen years later and I still jump out of bed every morning to do the work that Google sets out for us to accomplish!

—LINDSAY LEONE
Senior Business Lead at Google
LINKEDIN.COM/IN/LINDSAY-LEONE-VAN-HOUTEN-692535

108

We've heard you say "mentorship is a movement, not a moment." How did your mentors impact you as a US ambassador and as a senior corporate executive, and what is one piece of advice you would give girls today about identifying and approaching potential mentors of their own?

"

My mentors taught me how to own a room by speaking with facts. They helped me learn how to channel my intellect and unique ability to solve complex problems as a means to distinguish myself in multiple settings. Create a lifelong relationship with a wise and caring mentor who can help advise you at different stages throughout your professional journey.

—LISA GABLE
Former US Ambassador,
Wall Street Journal Bestselling Author, and CEO
in LINKEDIN.COM/IN/LISAGABLE

109

POPSUGAR is so on-trend

(and ahead of trends); what are some

roles or teams at the company that most

people wouldn't even know exist?

POPSUGAR has specialists in specific categories like entertainment, wellness, and beauty but many may not know that we also have a dedicated trending team that spends its time researching and writing stories about important, informative, and playful trends that will soon become topics on everyone's text chains, chat groups, and more. The teams also have early access to new product launches, shows, and books so we can recommend to our audience the next best obsessions.

—LISA SUGAR
Founder of POPSUGAR
LISAPOPSUGAR

What are smart ways girls can gain experience in architecture while still in high school or college, and is there one extra piece of industry advice you would share?

"

Practicing architecture entails making places and spaces that can positively affect the way in which we live. Since it is a very broad field that you can pursue from many perspectives, see if you enjoy learning about some of the following disciplines: art + design, architectural history, sustainability, community building, engineering, construction, and computer skills that involve three-dimensional fabrication. Contact numerous architectural offices, real estate developers, construction companies, governmental agencies, and design-build firms to try to secure any summer job where you can discover if the day-to-day workings of the field excite you. Listen to your inner voice and study architecture if you instinctively feel that it may be a good fit for you. Enter the field if the idea of becoming an architect makes your heart beat.

—LOUISE BRAVERMAN
Founding Principal at Louise Braverman Architect
LOUISEBRAVERMANARCH

111

What is your advice to girls interested in both medical research *and* space, and how can they gain early experience in fields like yours that seem so cool but also so specialized?

"

Study, or volunteer for, or get involved in things because you're *interested*. Stuff you're interested in is easy to work hard on— stuff you think you *have* to do isn't.

Say *yes* to fun and different opportunities when they come your way, even when they seem irrelevant or they're outside your comfort zone—you'll experience a wide range of things that will give you skills that you can use to work toward your goals. Failure is normal and OK! Don't beat yourself up—either keep trying, or pivot elsewhere. As one door closes, another opens.

—LUCIE LOW
Scientific Program Manager at the NIH,
National Center for Advancing Translational Sciences
DRLUCIEINTHESKY

You command entire ballrooms as a lead Christie's auctioneer—what is your advice to girls about how to walk into a room with enough confidence to stand out, even as a super new employee?

"

Take a deep breath, put your shoulders back, and smile. Remember that no one knows what you are supposed to say or do when you walk into a room except for you. Act confident and people will believe it!

—LYDIA FENET
Global Managing Director and Lead Charity Auctioneer at Christie's, and Author of THE MOST POWERFUL WOMAN IN THE ROOM IS YOU
LYDIAFENET

113

How did you decide to blend your interests in law and data/ technology, and what would you say to girls considering legal careers about options outside of traditional law firms?

"

I recognized that data and technology
presented an incredible opportunity to do
something bigger, something that could impact the
legal industry in a transformative way, improve how
people work, and make their lives easier. I love that
I've been able to create 'WOW' moments for legal
professionals, build products, take them to market,
and tell stories of innovation. I'm inspired and believe
that technology provides greater access to justice.

More epic advice? Always be true to yourself.
Create opportunities, don't wait for them. Develop a
network of mentors and sponsors. Be a platform
for change and to help others.

—LYDIA FLOCCHINI
CMO of SurePoint Technologies
in LINKEDIN.COM/IN/LYDIA-FLOCCHINI-1943506

114

How were you and Geena Davis able to change the faces we see on film, and how can girls starting their careers continue to end gender bias in media?

Data has always been the key to our success in making change for how women and girls are portrayed on screen. We have always used our research to support our advocacy and programs with the entertainment and media industry. And that's how in a relatively short period of time we were able to achieve gender parity for female lead characters in the top Nielsen-rated children's TV shows and the top one hundred largest-grossing family films in the US.

—MADELINE DI NONNO
President and CEO of the Geena Davis Institute on Gender in Media
⊙MADELINEDINONNO

You write about so many powerful women. What do young women not realize about power early enough in their careers?

"

What I wish more women knew about their power early in their careers is that they *have* power: the power of their voice. If you are in a room, you are there for a reason. Don't be shy and swallow your opinions; don't feel like you have to sit in the back of the room because you are new or younger. Take a seat at the table, ask questions, and raise your voice when appropriate. Your contributions matter.

—Maggie McGrath
Editor of Forbes Women
@MCGRATHMAG

116

As one of the first Latina journalists in many newsrooms and the founder of Futuro Media Group, what advice do you have for young women considering careers in journalism—especially if they are one or two of a few?

"

Young women! If you feel like journalism is
calling you, then you must listen to that voice.
You have to drown out the doubt. What's more
important is to convince yourself how important your
voice and perspective is in American journalism. It's
not easy but this is a profession that's about mission.
If you see your place in the world as wanting to leave
your impact then journalism is it. Believe in
your voice and believe in your power.

The world of journalism needs you desperately so
don't give up. You are part of a proud legacy from
Frederick Douglass to Jovita Idar to Ida B. Wells.

—MARIA HINOJOSA
President and Founder of Futuro Media,
Award-Winning Journalist, and Author
of ONCE I WAS YOU
🐦 MARIA_HINOJOSA

How did you feel when
you saw your first book title on
the *New York Times* Bestsellers List
(we would have freaked *all* the way out),
and what is a piece of mentor advice
you received that you can pass along to
aspiring authors?

"

The very first time I saw one of my books on the *New York Times* Bestseller List—with *THE ONLY WOMAN IN THE ROOM*—I felt a surge of immense gratitude. Not only deep appreciation for all the readers and booksellers and librarians and book clubs who were reading and recommending my novel, but for all the unknown historical women upon whose shoulders I stand and whose stories and legacies I attempt to excavate from the past and bring into the light of modern day. Without those women, I could not undertake the work I'm called to do, and I am eternally indebted to them.

When I think about the sort of advice I'd share with aspiring authors, it is those women again about whom I think when I recommend writers focus on topics about which they feel passionate (not simply what they think the market will bear); we owe it to all those women who couldn't pursue their callings because of societal limitations and expectations.

—Marie Benedict
New York Times Bestselling Author
AUTHORMARIEBENEDICT

118

"

Reimagining Barbie must have been a total dream job—what was that process like and what advice do you have for those of us who want to help other companies meet cultural moments like this?

"

Our goal is always to leave brands better than we find them, so evolving brands like Barbie for the next generation is a dream come true. There is a true intersection when you work on heritage brands on keeping what made them beloved in the first place while also ensuring they continue to be a reflection of current culture to remain relevant. My advice is simply to be a solid study of what is resonating in cultural context and to make sure that your brand is reflecting and embracing where the world is at—while ultimately remaining authentic. A brand's mission never goes out of style.

—MARISSA BECK
Head of Global Brand Communications for Mattel
LINKEDIN.COM/IN/MIBECK

119

What strategies from *YOUR FULLY CHARGED LIFE* are most applicable to girls entering the workforce now, and what is one piece of mentor advice you would pass on about finding true meaning in our work?

Have friends on the job. Good workplace relationships
are a key to helping us thrive. We're more motivated,
engaged, happier, and more satisfied with our jobs
when we have those connections. That 'work wife'
or 'work husband' could even increase your
employee satisfaction by 50 percent and
make work more worthwhile and fun.

—Meaghan B Murphy
Author of YOUR FULLY CHARGED LIFE,
Editor-in-Chief of Woman's Day, Co-Host of Off the
Gram Podcast, On-Air Personality
 MEAGHANBMURPHY

You talked at the Teen Vogue Summit about becoming a TikTok influencer through authenticity—what is your advice to girls starting digital content jobs, specifically about balancing creativity and authenticity?

"

I truly don't believe I am qualified enough to be advising anybody, simply because of the unpredictable nature of digital content creation, but I do believe any kind of creativity should be drawn from one's authenticity. What makes you unique as a person should inform the content you create. I believe using your identity and specific life experience as the core of your creativity is the route to making something truly one-of-a-kind and authentic to you.

—MEGHA RETHIN
Digital Creator
BOOTLEGMEGZ

121

What is going through your mind

in the moments before you leap out of a plane,

and how has skydiving allowed you to

highlight important women's issues?

"

Leaving the open door of an aircraft in flight seems impossible . . .
until you do it. So many things seem impossible, until we do them. This
experience of doing what we think we can't has consistently opened my mind
over the last twenty-five years and 11,000 jumps. It has built my confidence. It
has championed my creativity and business vision. It has nurtured my bravery
to be fully self-expressed in my relationships and in the world. It has driven me
to be a leader in all the ways I am. With a team of the most elite women in the
sport, we use the unique power of skydiving to capture attention both live
and on the largest media platforms. We use our voice and position
of privilege to stand for equality in all its forms.

—MELANIE CURTIS
Professional Skydiver and Cofounder
of Highlight Pro Skydiving Team
🅘 MELANIECURTIS11

122

What's the first thing we

should do before asking someone

to be our mentor?

"

Offer to be of service before you ask for anything.
That's how you build lasting relationships.

—MICHELE GHEE
CEO, EBONY and JET
IAMMICHELEGHEE

123

Why are early apprenticeships so vital to long-term career development, and how does FLIK's focus on female mentorship enhance career readiness even more?

"

Early apprenticeships and mentorship experiences are critical to long-term career development, especially for young women. Young women need to see women in leadership positions that resonate with their identity and passions to feel like they too can strive to break the glass ceiling and create their dream impact.

The female founders of today need to elevate the female founders of tomorrow so we can keep progressing toward gender equality.

—MICHELLE KWOK
Cofounder and CEO of FLIK
in LINKEDIN.COM/IN/MICHELLEBKWOK

124

How did your interests in astrophysics and aerospace engineering lead to your job at the International Space Station, and what do you want to tell girls interested in space science?

"

I had to try both astrophysics (study of planetary bodies) and aerospace engineering (study of building spacecrafts) to understand what they are and find where my interests are at. The answer was neither! I found that I'm interested in research (of all kinds) in space that cannot be done here on Earth, and that's what the ISS National Lab is about. It also helped me develop a systems level (or holistic) perspective.

Advice? Expand your horizon and explore other fields. Understanding the intertwined and complex world we live in is important in finding (a) new insights from seemingly unrelated/unexpected areas, as well as (b) your niche and its place in the whole picture.

—MIKI SODE
Commercial Innovation Manager at the International
Space Station US National Lab
 LINKEDIN.COM/IN/MIKISODE

125

What should we do if our career feels like it's zigzagging instead of moving in a straight line?

Don't be so focused on linear growth in your career. We sometimes get stuck thinking that the future happens without us, but go out there and make it yours. You can redesign your role and invent your own future.

—MIMI SWAIN
Chief Revenue Officer at Ring
LINKEDIN.COM/IN/MIMISWAIN

When did you know that
you were writing the right book
at exactly the right time, and do you
have any advice for other young
writers who want to be
catalysts for change?

"

I knew that writing *TIMELINES FROM BLACK HISTORY* was the right book to write when I found myself learning wonderful facts about Black figures in history I had previously known very little about, from finding out that Maya Angelou was San Francisco's first Black streetcar conductor to learning that the modern ironing board was invented by Sarah Boone. To discover these facts was incredibly empowering and enlightening at a time of immense trauma for the Black community. I would advise young writers who want to be catalysts for change to find their voice and find their reason—write from your heart, write about what makes you feel—whether that's anger and frustration or happiness, it's good to lean into those feelings and use the emotions to drive what you're trying to say and how.

—MIREILLE CASSANDRA HARPER
Author of TIMELINES FROM BLACK HISTORY,
Editor, and Sensitivity Reader
MIREILLECHARPER

127

At Unilever and now at Carta, you have helped companies have brave conversations about diversity and inclusion; what advice do you have for girls starting their careers who want to make sure similar conversations happen where they work?

"

Remember that your voice matters. My voice has become my superpower. Speak up for yourself, and speak for those who aren't ready to use their voices yet. It takes one person to speak up and start asking the tough questions, to begin to see a tidal wave of change happening across all our organizations.

—MITA MALLICK
Diversity, Equity, and Inclusion Thought Leader
in LINKEDIN.COM/IN/MITA-MALLICK-2B165822

How did you keep focused while training for the Olympics, and what advice would you give to girls eyeing paths to the Olympics in their sports?

"

While training for the Olympics, one thing that made me stay focused was creating a schedule with the outcome in mind. I worked backward creating it, and then checked back in to adjust it regularly.

I also had a great support system and people cheering me on for the Olympic Games. My gym even met me at the beach to run the sand dunes! Incredible people.

If you want to be an Olympian, I would say practice your craft and surround yourself with people who will push you forward and demand the best out of you every day.

— MONICA ABBOTT
Two-Time Olympic Silver Medalist, Team USA Softball (Pitcher)
 MONICAABBOTT

129

As a sports medicine physiatrist
and team physician to the 2019 World Cup
Champion US Women's National Soccer Team,
what is your advice to girls who want to
combine their love of sports with their skills
in science? How did you know you
would be able to do that?

"

Growing up I loved playing sports and I loved math and science.
I knew I was not going to be able to play competitive sports
for the rest of my life, but I loved being a part of a team and
having that special bond to work toward a common goal.
When I was discovering my path for what I wanted to do in
the future, I looked for careers that allowed for me to continue
to work with a team. As a Sports Medicine Physiatrist, I lead
a team of physical therapists, athletic trainers, researchers,
sports scientists, and nurses. I use my skills that I developed as a
captain of my sports teams to now lead these medical teams, and
I love every minute of it. Find what it is you love about sports
and look for fields in science, math, and technology that can give
you that same feeling! I feel lucky that I have a job that is all
about teamwork and working alongside others, because
it makes me sometimes feel like I'm still playing
alongside others on a field/court!

—MONICA RHO
Professor of Sports Medicine,
Team Physician for the US Women's National Soccer Team
MONICARHOMD

130

"
What is the best piece of advice you ever received in the beauty industry, and what piece of advice would you want those of us starting careers to keep as our screensaver?

"

'No amount of concealer or lipstick can mask an ugly heart.' My mom told me this when I first became a model so I would make sure to surround myself with kind people, no matter how they looked, warning me that surface beauty can sometimes draw you into someone who isn't good for you.

'Be kind, but be more than kind, interrupt unkindness!' This is a screensaver for life. It's so relevant today, but I've lived by this motto my entire life—another quote from my mom.

—MORGEN SCHICK
Ford Model and Author
MORGENSCHICK

131

What is the best piece of mentor advice you ever received from founding a company at 27, running the first women's TV network in Japan, or launching MyRegistry, and would you pass it on to girls today?

There are really no direct paths nor any shortcuts to success, but there are some basic common denominators you will find across all successful people. Hard work, commitment, and purpose will be at the core of what they do, no matter what field they are in. Having gone through several major career changes over the years, I found that I could continue to find success in new areas, as long as I continued to strive to be the best and do my best.

—NANCY LEE
President of MyRegistry
⧉MYREGISTRY

66

As the first woman ever to become head coach of a men's professional team in *any* sport, who was your most important mentor, and do you have any advice for girls considering careers in sports where they might also be a "first"?

66

My mentors in life were Muhammad Ali and Walt Frazier who played for the New York Knicks. I was blessed to play for Pat Riley, Pat Summit, and Marianne Stanley where I learned preparation, communication, and discipline at the highest level. They taught me how to develop my philosophy and how to take my players, individually and collectively, to the next level. This is a daily discipline to achieve success.

—NANCY LIEBERMAN
Basketball Hall of Famer, Two-Time Olympian, Former NBA Assistant Coach, Current Big3 Coach, and Philanthropist
@NANCYLIEBERMAN

133

How has joining the Rollettes wheelchair dance team expanded your network and community, and what do you want girls to know about the importance of strong community bonds in their careers?

"

Before joining the Rollettes, I didn't have any disabled friends and, to be honest, I wasn't looking for any. But meeting like-minded women who understood living life with a disability as a young adult opened my eyes to a community that is supportive, close-knit, and resilient. I would not be where I am today—graduate student and disability advocate— without learning from those who came before me and having the encouragement of my peers.

—NATALIE FUNG
Member of the Rollettes Wheelchair Dance Team
NATLEEF

What has pro parkour athlete training taught you about goal setting, and what do you want other girls to know about setting demanding goals for themselves early on in their careers?

"

Being a girl in the parkour culture that is mostly dominated by males means for me basically that you have to grow some lady balls! I challenge myself to train with the guys instead of only with girls or training alone, because by doing that I have to work harder, to get stronger just to keep up with them. Because this sport challenges you to overcome fears, both mental and physical, you will gain more confidence and trust in yourself after every challenge you do. I believe every girl should try that—it will benefit you in the rest of your life journey!

—Noa Diorgina Man
Red Bull Freerun/Parkour Athlete
NOA_DIORGINA

What is your advice to girls who want to bring their first film to life and, specifically, how should they think about early financing?

"

To get your first film made, focus on raising awareness and creating a compelling story about your project very early on, with social media, behind the scenes, crowdfunding, bloggers, etc. Funding is all about relationships, so go everywhere that people who are passionate about the topic of your film are (events, conferences, etc.) to build those relationships early on.

—NORA POGGI
Director and Producer of the Award-Winning
Documentary SHE STARTED IT
NORA.POGGI

You hold the Guinness World Record for "The Most Live Radio Interviews Conducted in 24 Hours"—what makes a great interview, and what is your advice to girls hoping to crush our first job interviews?

"

What makes a great interview are a few key components:
(1) Know your subject; people love when you have taken the time and delved into their career/life/their company! Trust me—most do not!
(2) Arrive early—show that you're conscious of their time.
(3) Look like you want the job and look professional for their business.
(4) Smile and be confident—you've got this!

—PAVLINA OSTA
Author of 20 THINGS EVERY MOTIVATED
20-SOMETHING SHOULD KNOW
PAVLINAOSTA

How did your career path lead
to your current role at TikTok, and
what is one piece of mentor advice
you would pass on to girls entering
the media/advertising and tech
spaces right now?

"

I have had a non-traditional path as I started my career in investment banking and then transitioned to the media, and eventually ad tech space, post-business school. The common thread for me has been working in entrepreneurial, fast-paced environments, building up my strategic and operational skill set, and finding ways to deliver business impact and influence revenue. Additionally, in the last several years, I have been focused on sharpening my management skills, gaining global experience, and creating stakeholder alignment, all of which are critical to my role at TikTok.

My advice? Get an executive sponsor. This is one of the biggest learnings I have had in my career—*find your people.* This certainly does not happen overnight; it requires building relationships, proving yourself, and working hard. However, once you do, find that senior person who wants you on their team and will support and advocate for you.

—PRITI DALAL
Head of Global Brand Strategy, Platform at TikTok
in LINKEDIN.COM/IN/PRITI-DALAL

What is it like to interview at NASA and with the International Space Station National Lab, and what is your advice to those of us preparing for careers in space science?

"

The things people do in space are often unprecedented and need an abundance of creative thought. We are always doing something new in space and therefore encountering new problems. So when interviewing, don't be afraid to tell a story about your own creative problem-solving skills.

In addition to staying curious, I would encourage young people to seek out advocates or sponsors—I would suggest finding more than one. These are people who not only could advise on how to build the career you want in space, but can also help to network and find opportunities to gain experience. Get to know the people at an internship or space event, send an email and set up a one-on-one phone call. There are plenty of people in the space sector who want to help others succeed. You only need to find them and strike up a conversation.

—RACHEL CLEMENS
Axiom Space, Former Commercial Innovation Manager at the International Space Station US National Lab
in LINKEDIN.COM/IN/RACHEL-CLEMENS-PHD

Why are all-female networks and communities so important, and why are our twenties not too young to be thinking about forging those bonds in our professional lives?

"

Women face a unique set of challenges in the workplace, so having these networks and communities can prove invaluable when looking for support and mentorship. In your toughest moments, being able to tap into your network for expert advice can be extremely helpful, knowing you don't have to go at it alone.

You're never too young to start trying to build a network of professional relationships. Often, building strong relationships with your peers in entry-level positions can help lead to fostering an organic network that will grow as you grow.

—REBECCA MINKOFF
Founder, Designer, Podcast Host, and Author of FEARLESS
@REBECCAMINKOFF

What advice do you have for STEM girls who worry they are not a good fit for a particular job?

You are not right for every position and every position isn't right for you. Stay true to what makes you happy, work hard, be proud of your skills, and don't try to change yourself to fit into the mold of an organization. Wait for an organization that wants to make space for the special skill set you bring to the job.

—SAMANTHA THORSTENSEN
International Space Station, US National Lab
Education Project Manager
LINKEDIN.COM/IN/SAMANTHA-THORSTENSEN

"How can we—at these early stages in our careers—make sure that DEI principles are incorporated into the corporate cultures where we work? How can we help bring these ideals forward as the most junior team members?"

A simple thing anyone can do to support and promote DEI principles into the corporate cultures where they work is to include their pronouns after their name in their signature. This is a powerful way to normalize the conversation around gender identity, demonstrate that they value inclusivity, and help your colleagues refrain from making assumptions about other people's gender.

—SANDHYA JAIN PATEL
Cofounder and Culture Producer at SRC Partners
LINKEDIN.COM/IN/SANDHYA-JAIN-PATEL

142

What was your specific career path to become a judge, and what is one piece of valuable mentor advice that you received along the way?

> "
>
> I have always thought of a limitation as a challenge. Never tell me that I cannot do something unless you want me to try it. I refuse to be pigeonholed as anything other than a hardworking, competent, and reliable professional. Neither gender nor race should be an impediment to me accomplishing my goals.

—SANDRA AMMANN
Senior US District Judge,
First Woman on the US District Court for the Southern District of Ohio
✉ SANDRA_BECKWITH@OHSD.USCOURTS.GOV

What do you see as the future of retail technology, and how can girls acquire some of the skills we need before we enter the workforce?

"

Retail is ever-changing, but the future is technology that helps brands connect more authentically to the consumer and retains them, predicting timely trends, forecasting inventory needs for improved sell-through and profitability, and has the ability to break through the 'noise' via innovative digital marketing strategies.

Learning specific skills is one thing, but if you don't understand the industry at large, or how each functional department works, a role can become siloed. Learning through platforms such as Fashion Launchpad, a user can gain knowledge across all disciplines, which leads to more informed and thoughtful solutions.

—Sandra Campos
Retail and Tech CEO, Founder of Fashion Launchpad
@SANDRACAMPOSNYC

What do colleges *really* want

to know about us, and what makes the

best applications stand out?

"

Admissions officers want to discover something different about you. Something interesting. The best applications showcase your true self and have a special spark that only you can make colleges see. Discovering who you truly are and revealing that to colleges is what I teach students in my book *SOUNDBITE*.

—Sara Harberson
Founder of Application Nation and Author
of SOUNDBITE: THE ADMISSIONS SECRET THAT GETS YOU
INTO COLLEGE AND BEYOND
⊙SARAHARBERSON

145

"

What is your advice to

girls who are hesitant to show

vulnerability at work?

"

In the world of business I was always taught 'never let them see you sweat,' which translated to never let them see you cry, question yourself, or be vulnerable in any way while working. The expectation is that you are always confident, always on your game, always climbing. The problem is, that's not human.

Hiding vulnerability all the time does not allow you to bring your whole authentic self to the job. It does not allow you to grow because you may be too afraid to show you don't know something, or to ask questions. Just remember—there is a reason you were hired. You had something special they valued. So allow your whole being to be present at work. When you do, you will feel more comfortable in your own skin, and confidence will be a natural by-product.

—Sara Sidner
CNN National and International Correspondent
 SARASIDNERTV

146

Why is collective knowledge crucial

to workplace success, and how can we leverage

networks early as brand-new employees?

The whole is always going to be stronger than the sum of its parts.
Collective knowledge brings in experience and viewpoints from a
more diverse group of people, and diverse input is always
going to make decision-making stronger.

The single best way to leverage networks for new employees is to
ask for help when you need it. Young women are afraid to ask for
help because they think it makes them look inexperienced or weak,
but the research shows that people like and respect you *more*
when you make reasonable requests. It's the best way to develop
closer bonds with others, and then of course you should
pay it forward and help someone else.

—SARAH ALLEN-SHORT
Vice President of Marketing at Give and Take
LINKEDIN.COM/IN/SARAHALLENSHORT

What was your job like as the
first lawyer at Etsy, and what
advice would you pass on to girls
considering the idea
of law school?

"

As the first lawyer at Etsy, my role was a cross between a ping-pong player and a firefighter. When an issue was bounced to me, I'd include tangible and strategic business advice when paddling it back. Additionally, I'd find and smother tiny fires before they could grow into something harmful. Lawyers are typically risk averse; but in a startup, you must quiet your legal brain, turn up your business senses, absorb all aspects of the company, and take appropriate risks.

Attending law school is (obviously) a big decision. I suggest writing down why you're considering this path and what you hope to do, long-term. Then, reach out to people who have similar careers and ask to pick their brains. What do they do? What advice do they have? The practice of law is vast, challenging, and is always changing; it can be valuable to hear from people who are a few steps ahead of where you hope to be.

You own your career. Your career is your responsibility (it isn't the responsibility of the place you work, a loved one, your mentor, etc.). It is never too early (or too late) to call yourself an expert and dive into an area of interest. Create your own opportunities. Find the community and thought leaders in your selected subject matter, contribute to the conversation, publicize your accomplishments, and keep learning. Oh, and be kind.

—SARAH FEINGOLD
Cofounder of The Fourth Floor, First Attorney at Etsy
 LINKEDIN.COM/IN/SARAHFEINGOLD

148

What if we don't know exactly what

we want to do or where we want to work yet?

In other words, what happens if we can't

pick one specific career path?

"

Focus on skills you excel in, then apply these to industries or problems you're passionate about. Remember that a job is not forever, and you aren't defined by your title or the company you work for. Just like life, careers are about the journey, not the destination—so do what you love, but when what you love changes, don't be afraid to change with it.

—SARAH WILSON
Pro Skier to Biomechanical Engineer to Robotics Engineer
SARAHINTHESNOW

As a recent Yale graduate, what was the biggest challenge you faced when transitioning to the National Women's Hockey League, and what is your advice to younger players about sticking with their sport?

The biggest challenge I faced when transitioning to the NWHL was finding the balance between the real world and my sport. Upon graduation, the world lies in front of you. But, as women, we must not only continue to conquer in our sport but in the workforce as well. I had to learn to balance my work life and my sport.

—Saroya Tinker
Pro Hockey Player in NWHL Toronto Six
SAROYATINKER71

"

For girls who love art/design *and* tech, where do

you see the future of interior design going,

and what kinds of tech developments do you

think will impact that direction?

"

The future of interior design will continue to merge
art and technology. Advances in 3D technology will allow
designers to be able to effortlessly turn their visions into
photorealistic, digital visuals that allow clients to truly
imagine the possibilities and bring these visions to life.

—SHANNA TELLERMAN
Founder and CEO of Modsy
in LINKEDIN.COM/IN/SHANNATELLERMAN

151

How did you know when the moment was right to move to your role at Shutterfly, and what is your advice to girls who are waiting for "the perfect time" to make a big career move?

> ❝
>
> I believe that life presents opportunities when the time is right, and you have to grab them. I felt that I had made a significant impact at Smule and got my functions to run and operate smoothly and built a strong team and led the company to profitability—that's when I knew it was time to embrace a new challenge and have the ability to make an impact elsewhere. You know in your gut it's time!

—SHARON SEGEV
Chief Legal and People Officer at Shutterfly
LINKEDIN.COM/IN/SHARON-SEGEV-6834651

152

You were the face of Fiverr,
the company that then acquired your
first business; what did that feel like and
what do you want girls to know about
building their own personal brands?

"

Both were 'OMG, this is beyond my wildest dreams' moments for me. In the Fiverr ad campaign, I was showcased as an expert in my field— it gave me credibility and exposure *(literally, my face was all over the subway)* in a city where I was building my business. In many ways, Fiverr helped me to establish my personal brand. The image of me in the ad became my calling card—the Sharon in the photo is confident, knowledgeable, professional, and poised. She is someone you'd hire to help you with digital marketing. That campaign communicates a clear representation of how I want to be seen professionally.

When you think about your own personal brand, identify what traits, values, attitudes, or vibes you want to be known for and how you want people to remember you. Make a list of what you're really good at, or reasons why people engage with you: Are you a good friend, are you a great listener, are you a problem solver, are you always full of great ideas? Then connect your unique qualities to the impact that you want to have on the world.

Find ways to get your brand out there so that people can get to know you, be inspired by you, and above all, remember you.

—SHARON THONY
CEO of SLT Consulting and
Host of Modern Minorities Podcast
🅾 SHARON_THONY

153

What are some unique or unusual STEM careers you have seen through your work at the Intrepid that girls might not even think to pursue?

"

Some unusual careers at the Intrepid Museum are aircraft restoration specialists and artifact curators. The aircraft restorers help to take care of the planes in our collection. They restore and rebuild planes that we obtain from other people and organizations to include in the Intrepid's collections. Curators of the Intrepid Museum also have an awesome job because they collect and organize really old things that are related to Intrepid's history. They make sure these objects are kept safe in temperature-controlled rooms and are rotated throughout our collections. These artifacts are special because they help to tell the unique stories of those who served aboard the ship.

—SHAY SALEEM
Cofounder of GOALS for Girls,
Intrepid Sea, Air, and Space Museum
LINKEDIN.COM/IN/SHIHADAH-SHAY-S-BA76409

"

You have been called a Chief Troublemaker;

why should girls not be afraid to cause trouble

in order to bring change in the work world?

The rules of the workplace were written by men, for men
over 100 years ago. Sometimes you have to break the rules
and create new ones *and* sometimes you need to
be a troublemaker to do that!

Always own your voice and never be afraid to use it! The
future of leadership in the workplace is Female!

—SHELLEY ZALIS
CEO, The Female Quotient
LINKEDIN.COM/IN/SHELLEYZALIS

155

Why is quality sleep vital to succeeding in the work world?

"

Quality sleep is vital to your leadership, as it gives you emotional resilience, as well as mental and physical strength. It is a key source of energy, clarity, and confidence. Achieving deep rest on a consistent basis, especially during challenging times, has enabled me to lead with empathy and courage. Sleeping well supports your ability to stay present and engaged, to be your best self at work and in life. Quality sleep will lead to a kinder, more gracious world with greater unity and joy.

—SHELLY IBACH
CEO of Sleep Number
SHELLYIBACH

156

What should entrepreneurial girls of color know about accessing capital for new ventures, and what is one piece of pitch advice you want girls everywhere to remember?

66

I want girls everywhere to know that your voice grows as you grow. If you see something, know that it is OK to say something. Say how you feel. Say what you want. Say who you are. Say out loud the change that you want to see in your world. Pitching your business is articulating what your idea is, what it does, why it matters, who it matters to, and how it will make money. Don't be afraid to express that your ideas have a return on investment. Whether that return is valuable in capital or community empowerment, it is valuable nonetheless. Not everyone will see you coming. View any levels of invisibility as a superpower. When people don't see you coming that means you can come from any direction and win! You got this! Remember, entrepreneurship is a boxing match and you know how to stay light on your feet!

—Shelly Omilâdè Bell
Founder and CEO of Black Girl Ventures
@IAMSHELLYBELL

157

What do you want girls

everywhere to know

about ambition?

Hard work and ambition aren't enough.
You have to be strategic, intentional,
and take help from others.

—Shellye Archambeau
CEO, Silicon Valley Leader, Board Member, and Author of
UNAPOLOGETICALLY AMBITIOUS
@SHELARCHAMBEAU

How do the skills learned in academic environments like Barnard transfer from the classroom to the boardroom; in other words, what do alumni say about the impact of an all-women's education in their professional lives?

"

Academic environments that are focused
on educating and empowering women, like Barnard
College at Columbia University, ease the transition from
the classroom to the boardroom by providing unfettered
access to female mentors and female-majority working
groups who help our graduates build networks for career
advancement. In particular, research strongly suggests
that female mentors are needed to patch the leaky STEM
pipeline, enabling women to reach parity with men in
these highly competitive, well-paying jobs. After just one
year of attendance, students at all-women's colleges are
far more likely than their counterparts at co-ed
colleges to abandon the belief that men are
better suited for leadership positions.

—Sian Beilock
President of Barnard College
LINKEDIN.COM/IN/SIANLEAHBEILOCK

How did you start creating content for companies like HOKA ONE ONE, BetterHelp, and Zappos, and how do you keep your ideas consistently creative and fresh?

"

Creating content that I liked first and was true to me—this really only started happening when I started sharing my writing versus just sharing photos—and then brands started reaching out for ways that we could work to create content together. Many times we work with their brand values and create content from there. How do I keep ideas consistently creative and fresh? I think inspiration is always around—it's just a matter of getting quiet enough to hear it.

—SOPHIA JOAN SHORT
Digital Content Creator and Author
SOPHIA.JOAN.SHORT

160

In our job interviews, what are a few ways we can ask about diversity and inclusion culture, or how companies address unconscious bias?

"

Ask the following questions: How have you addressed pay equity within your company? What employee resource groups does your company have and what is the purpose of allowing them to exist? To help fast-track my introduction to the company culture, what action would you recommend I take upon starting in my role?

—STACEY GORDON
Executive Advisor and Diversity Strategist at Rework Work
REWORKWORK

161

How did you know when it was time to walk away from a job that wasn't working for you in order to launch your passion project in sports, and how did you know Voice In Sport would be successful?

"

I built businesses for fourteen years at Nike because I was passionate about the power of sport and leadership. As CEO of a global fashion brand, I learned that leadership without passion wasn't enough. I was searching for a way to bring my two passions together—sport and developing future leaders. I knew if I created a company that reflected its mission and vision inside and outside of the company that elevated girls in sport and women leaders beyond an 'initiative,' then it would be successful. When you combine passion and purpose—you will drive real change— and that is what we are doing at Voice In Sport.

—STEF STRACK
Founder and CEO of Voice In Sport
VOICEINSPORT

What are some smart ways girls can get early experience as makeup artists, and is there a piece of mentor advice from your own experience that you would pass on to us?

"

Starting out in the makeup community can be quite difficult because it is extremely competitive. But that should not stop you from your passion. What makes you different is what's going to make you stand out.

It took me quite a while to figure that out, but now I take pride in being a 'quadriplegic' makeup artist. It has given me a brand much larger than being simply in the makeup community. It has given me the purpose to strive for more inclusivity when it comes to the product packaging and support from brands. It was Tyra Banks who stunned me with advice like 'your hands are your brand,' that drove me to become successful in the makeup community and gave me the confidence to show the world that our 'disability' does not define us, and that we are all beautiful in our own amazing ways!

—STEPH AIELLO
Makeup Artist and Disability Advocate
YOUWALKIGLIDE

163

"

What is one piece of mentor advice you want new graduates to know about making the big transition from campus life to office life?

##

In college, you're used to splitting your time each day between many different pursuits: multiple classes, extracurriculars, a campus job, athletics, and more. So it can be a big change to get used to focusing on the same thing all day, every day at your job. Create variation for yourself by making plans outside of work, scheduling lunches with different coworkers, and finding ways to make your workday feel like it includes distinct parts, to break up this new monotony.

—STEPHANIE KAPLAN LEWIS
Cofounder and CEO, Her Campus Media
STEPHKAPLEWIS

164

As an actress, producer, entrepreneur, and philanthropist,

in which role do you feel like you've had your bravest

moments, and what would you tell girls about finding,

and cultivating, our own courage at work?

"

I would tell any young woman the following: you do not have to be someone's nice girl. I spent far too much time people-pleasing when I embarked on my professional life. I turned myself into knots filling the needs of others and fitting in to other agendas in an attempt to make myself useful, valuable, and agreeable. I never asked myself, 'Stephanie, what do you need to fulfill your goals? How is what you are doing right now adding up to what you most want?' And in doing so, I lost a lot of time and my confidence eroded. Turning forty helped put the brakes on that behavior, but I wish someone had said that to me when I graduated from school.

—STEPHANIE MARCH
Actress, Founder, and Philanthropist
@MARCHSTEPHANIE

165

How does your WWE role change depending

on the audience in front of you, and is there a piece

of advice you would pass on to girls about having a

job that requires different personas at different times?

"

The number one rule of communication is to know your audience.
How I deliver a message as a villainous television character to thousands
in an arena and millions watching at home is very different than how
I communicate when I'm pitching the World Wrestling Entertainment
(WWE) brand to potential partners, or speaking to the Connecticut
delegation of Special Olympics athletes as honorary chairperson.
But the best advice I can give is to always tell a story. Maya Angelou is
quoted as saying, 'People will forget what you said, people will forget
what you did, but people will never forget how you made them feel.'
Tell a story and make people feel, then you will engender the
connection you need to get your point across.

—STEPHANIE MCMAHON
Chief Brand Officer at WWE
🐦 STEPHMCMAHON

How long can it take for writers to get their

first sketch on *Saturday Night Live*, and

what is your advice to girls who want

to write sketch comedy?

❝

It can take a long time for a writer to get their first sketch on. I didn't have my first sketch on until April of my first year; there were only a few shows left in the season, and I was freaking out that I wouldn't get anything on the show. Fortunately I kept pushing myself and eventually I produced something that worked. My advice to girls who want to write sketch comedy is to perform and write as much as you can, get the repetitions in, and you will watch yourself get better and better. Surround yourself with people who will inspire you and make you want to be funnier. Make things with friends!

—SUDI GREEN
Writer at Saturday Night Live
 SUDIGREEN

167

What was the path that led to your current role at SpaceX, and what advice (classes, internships, experience) do you have for girls looking to land jobs in space technology someday?

"

I actually changed my major in college a couple of times and worked in several different jobs and research labs until I started working in Dr. David Miles' Space Physics Research Lab at the University of Iowa. I realized there that I wanted to work in space because it was something that I looked forward to doing every day.

My advice to girls looking to land jobs in space technology is: explore all the possibilities and take on projects that really excite you. Whether it be through working at a research lab at your university or a personal project, always follow what excites you. Your passion and excitement will lead the way.

—SUMAN SHERWANI
*Avionics Integration and Operations
Engineer at SpaceX*
ⓘ ASTRO_SUMAN

When did you first know
you wanted to go into engineering,
and what should we know about
aerospace career paths at large
aerospace companies?

> ❝

As a young girl, I always wanted to fly—literally. I loved the sky and was curious about what else was out there. I would stand outside with a blanket tied at my neck, my arms straight out, and once in the ready position, I would try to take off! My parents would come out and encourage me to fly another way, but not once did they tell me I couldn't fly. So, it is no surprise that I became an aerospace engineer. Now, I am flying, just a little differently than I originally imagined.

What should you know about aerospace career paths?

Explore. There are so many opportunities in aerospace. Learn about them, talk to people, intern, and try different roles! You do not have to have it all figured out. Life is a journey! Explore, be curious, ask questions, and enjoy every moment of finding what excites you. *Network.* It can be challenging being the youngest, the only woman, or the only minority in the room. Find new opportunities to expand your network and have someone who can support you in meetings. It is a lot easier to speak up when you have a hype person in the room!

Know Your Facts. Who can challenge your abilities when you are well prepared and factual? No one can dispute the facts! Do your best to always be prepared so they know you for your technical abilities. *Own Your Career.* There are enough people in the world who will tell you *no* or try to stop you. You don't need to be one of them. Believe in yourself and remember it's your future to determine, not theirs.

—SYDNEY HAMILTON
Aerospace Structures Stress Manager at Boeing
 SEESYDSOAR

169

66

What is the most important thing for us to focus on in our early internships and first jobs? What is key to stay clear about?

66

Focus on building healthy and vibrant relationships whether they are peer-to-peer or with mentors you meet during your internship. And then cultivate them by staying in touch, sharing developments, and asking about ways that you can support them. These will likely be relationships you carry with you throughout your career. This a great time to connect with people who share your interests, who have skill sets you can learn from, and who you can form community with as your career journey progresses over time.

—TAI BEAUCHAMP
TV Host and Cofounder of Brown Girl Jane
TAIBEAU

170

Why do Girls Who Code alums have a network for life, and how can girls entering the tech workforce reach out to that community?

Sisterhood and mentorship are key parts of the work we do at Girls Who Code, and it's something that truly reflects in my own values. We don't just teach our girls how to code, we create a community of girls passionate about the tech and coding field. We want our alumni to feel supported as they move through their educational and professional careers.

Having the support of a community is essential, and their peers, teachers, and other connections they make during Girls Who Code are just a phone call, email, or LinkedIn message away, long after they finish Girls Who Code's programming.

—Tarika Barrett, PhD
CEO of Girls Who Code
GIRLSWHOCODE

171

When people think about careers in space they usually picture astronauts, but what are other jobs in the space industry that girls should know about, and how can we prepare for them?

"

A love for science and space doesn't have to end just because you didn't become a scientist or an astronaut. Marketing, communications, social media, graphic design, etc. are important skills to have to maintain what is now a thriving business and a growing economy in space. Speak up, network, mingle with people who don't think like you, have lots of conversations because you never know where your creativity may come from nor who you may meet. Never stop learning new skills. If you don't see a role for yourself at the time, create one for yourself for the future!

—TERE RILEY
Senior Manager Brand Strategy,
Redwire Space
TERERILEY

172

What was your career path into sports journalism,

and what do you want today's girls to know

about getting a cleat in the door at ESPN?

"

My career path to this profession actually started as a hobby, as writing and debating about sports was always something I did for fun. I took advantage of the opportunities that I was given, and when no opportunities were available, I created them. From hosting an Internet radio show, to believing in myself and applying for a job at ESPN, to networking with everyone I met along the way, I am one of the few people who was able to turn my passion into my profession.

For any young woman interested in working at ESPN, or anywhere in the sports industry: yes, it is a man's world but we have certainly found our place in it. Align yourself with a company that is open to the ideas, the values, and understands the importance of women. Continue to work hard, do not compromise yourself or your morals, and do not be intimidated by those in the room who may not look like you. It is your uniqueness and authenticity that will set you apart and that is your strength to conquer whatever you set out to do in the sports industry.

—TERRIKA FOSTER-BRASBY
Producer at ESPN
SHEKNOWSSPORTS_

173

What is the best way to ask someone to be your mentor, and what is one mistake we should try to avoid when asking for career mentorship?

"

When seeking a mentor the best advice I can give is first, be sure to choose a mentor who is not only skilled in a profession you're interested in, but they've also shown interest in sharing their wisdom with others. A great way to test-drive whether a mentor relationship will work is to first ask them to join you for a thirty-minute coffee or tea meeting.

Avoid saying things like, 'I want to pick your brain' or 'I want to learn from you'; those are very general statements. Instead, have your sixty-second elevator pitch prepared about who you are and what you've done to build your skills to date. Then share what key areas you're looking to grow and how you believe their unique background can get you there.

To find a mentor, identify key areas in your life where you are looking to advance; once that is established think of people in your life who are crushing it in those areas. It doesn't matter if it's a direct connection or someone you haven't even met.

Now that you have that list, determine who might be willing to share that knowledge with you. They may have proven this by giving speeches, lectures, volunteering, or even mentoring other people. Schedule a conversation where you express your interest, purpose for mentorship, and willingness to do the work.

Then you are on your way!

—TIANA DAVIS KARA
Diversity, Equity, Inclusion, and Belonging Lead at Nextdoor
LINKEDIN.COM/IN/TIANADAVISKARA

174

How has your sport enabled you to break barriers and empower other athletes, and what advice do you have for girls hoping to break barriers of their own through professional sports?

"

My sport has allowed me to break barriers and empower other athletes by giving me the opportunity to meet and build so many relationships with people around the world. Golf has also taught me so much about life and how there are so many lessons that can be learned through sport, such as patience, perseverance, honesty, integrity, and respect. Through playing golf my entire life I have been able to meet many influential people who range from CEOs, brands, mentors, celebrities, and more, which has led me to bigger opportunities and larger platforms to speak from.

My best advice that I can offer to anyone who is hoping to break barriers is to make strong relationships with everyone you come across. Who you know and that first impression you make can catapult you into the next best thing! My second piece of advice would be to leave your sport better than the way you were introduced to it, and that every voice matters and you can make a difference through power of action.

—TISHA ALYN
Golf Media Personality
TISHAALYN

175

What are three pieces of advice
you would give to aspiring animators
who dream about someday interning
or working at Pixar?
Bonus Q: How many Pixar films
have you worked on to date?

"

To aspiring animators: (1) Study acting; great animation is a deep examination and understanding of subtle gestures and reactions. Be surgical; focus on the study of weight and physicality: how things actually move and behave, not just caricatured movement but movement in real life. (2) Drawing! You don't have to be good at drawing but doing it certainly helps! So many things associated with it directly translate to animation—lines of action, silhouette, strong poses, etc. (3) Curate a great short demo reel, only including your best work; we don't need to see everything you can do, just the best you can do. Context and growth are very important and clearly understanding why you chose certain work shows a sophistication and shift in thinking and approach.

To aspiring producers: (1) Embrace and value all of your experiences (professional, volunteer, interests, family) and leverage and present them as the rich, whole package that is you. (2) Craft a compelling cover letter; this is where you reveal yourself, not where you sell yourself.

Always present your experience (the what) in your résumé but unmask and unfold yourself (the why) in your cover. (3) Producing is a 'leadership craft' and leadership at Pixar centers a lot around observation, empathy, and quick and accurate judgment calls. Learn how to 'read a room' and pick up on the subtleties of your audience and team.

Bonus A: I've worked directly on ten Pixar films.

—TRICIA ANDRES
Recruiter at Pixar
 TRICIAMANDRES

176

We love your advice about looking and feeling great on a budget; what is your advice to girls entering the workforce who want to achieve authentic beauty without blowing their paycheck?

"

My advice for looking great in the workplace without breaking the bank would be to head to your favorite stores' sale racks before you browse anything else. My mom always taught me to start in the sale area because you'll never know what you'll actually find. Also thrift and consignment stores have amazing selections of blazers, dresses, and trousers that are work appropriate and super affordable.

—Tyla-Lauren Gilmore
Digital Creator
TYLAUREN

Why is it so important to be really prepared, or even overprepared, for every single meeting?

If you're prepared, you'll be less nervous. If you're prepared, you won't waste your or others' time. If you're prepared, you'll do your best. If you're prepared, you'll impress.

—TYRA BANKS
Entrepreneur and Supermodel
TYRABANKS

How did you know, after going through years of law

school and law practice, that it was the right time

to leave and pursue your passion?

How did you know the leap would be worth the risk?

66

If you're dissatisfied with your career, don't be afraid to pivot. I left my
career as a lawyer to become a professional baker and food personality,
and it was the best decision I've ever made. It's not too late
to make a change and create the life you want.

—VALLERY LOMAS
Lawyer Turned Baker, Winner of ABC's
The Great American Baking Show, and Author of
LIFE IS WHAT YOU BAKE IT
🄾 FOODIEINNEWYORK

179

What is one piece of advice about workplace

fashion that you want girls everywhere to

know before we take that first job

or internship?

"

My mindset is 'supermodel CEO.' Never apologize for wanting to be *all*. Your job/career (no matter what it is, doctor, teacher, social worker . . .) is your runway for fashion and your individual look! You get *one* shot at this first impression. I always think about Kelly McGillis in *TOP GUN* when she walked down the aisle in the pencil skirt and bomber jacket, blonde hair blowing. She turned around and completely disarmed the room! How you walk through the door is critical! Wear an outfit that drives all attention to your face and complement with your hair and makeup so you look and feel legit and confident. If you wear what makes you feel gorgeous, you'll slay dragons!

—Veronica Miele Beard
Cofounder and Co-CEO of Veronica Beard
🄾 VERONICABEARD

180

INDEX

ACKNOWLEDGMENTS

Some books take a village—this one took an epic squad. There is no way a project like this happens without acres of smart friends, a slew of keen-eyed advisors, an army of awe-inspiring women, and a mob of curious girls.

Here we go. Endless thanks…

… to the girlfriends, sisters, cousins, and champions for brainstorming and for sharing your networks with a generosity I will never be able to repay—even though I will try.

… to Heather Terrell for making me draw up a blue sky list five years ago, and to Heather Shamsai for holding me to it.

… to Beth O'Connell, for fielding all my questions, for knowing all the answers, and for everything we're going to do next.

… to Jonathan Merkh, Justin Batt, Jennifer Gingerich, and Lauren Ward at Forefront Books and Worth Books, for the stellar team of editors, designers, and proofreaders you brought to the party, to Elysse Wagner and Jackie Karneth at Books Forward for making sure everyone knew about the party, and to Simon & Schuster for throwing the party.

… to Sharon Thony, Nina Pearl, Maia Hariton, and Carla Monticelli at SLT for the social and website wizardry you keep dreaming up.

… to my parents for teaching me to ask hard questions and run down the answers, and to my in-laws for being a second set of lifelong role models.

… to Sophia and Lawrence for being the best kids ever, even though I said that absolutely no one in this house was getting an Être tattoo.

… to my husband, Lawrence, who stole my heart before I ever started work and has kept it safe all these years.

… to the epic women who answered girls' questions with brilliance, candor, wit, and clarity, and encouraged them to ask more, and

… to the girls whose questions started this book in the first place. Keep raising those hands and never lower your standards.

THE GIRLS

You asked. So we asked. Thank you for contributing such smart and insightful questions for *The Epic Mentor Guide*. We are endlessly inspired by you.

Aalaa R., ONTARIO

Abby J., MASSACHUSETTS

Akshita B., UNITED ARAB EMIRATES

Alex Jayne G., CALIFORNIA

Alexa K., FLORIDA

Alexis D., SOUTH CAROLINA

Alli F., WASHINGTON

Allison K., NEW JERSEY

Alyshba A., NEW YORK

Alyshia H., NEW YORK

Alyzza C., NEW YORK

Amber C., NEW JERSEY

Angelique M., NEW JERSEY

Annalise P., TEXAS

Arianna G., ONTARIO

Ashley K., NEW JERSEY

Ashley T., TORONTO

Audrey B., VIRGINIA

Banan G., ILLINOIS

Bethany W., NEW JERSEY

Breanna C., PUERTO RICO

Brianna D., NEW JERSEY

Brianne J., CALIFORNIA

Bridget B., FLORIDA

Cameron S., NEW JERSEY

Caroline G., VIRGINIA

Caroline P., MARYLAND

Caroline T., VIRGINIA

Cassie G., FLORIDA

Celia B., NEW JERSEY

Chelsea K., VIRGINIA

Chloé B., NEW YORK

Cortlyn C., TEXAS

Courtney L., NEW JERSEY

Dahlia G., NEW JERSEY

Daniella Z., NEW JERSEY

Danielle S., VIRGINIA

Darby L.S., NEW YORK

Devangana R., ILLINOIS

Dorcas O., VIRGINIA

Elizabeth S., NEW YORK

Elizabeth S., NEW JERSEY

Elle C., NORTH CAROLINA

Emily D., NEW YORK

Fiona S., MARYLAND

Foziea G., ILLINOIS

Gabriella R., NEW JERSEY

Gabriella W., FLORIDA

Georgia P., TEXAS

Glori M., NEW JERSEY

Hadassah F., ISRAEL

Hannah H., MARYLAND

Hannah R., NEW JERSEY

Hillary A., NEW YORK

Ilana F., ILLINOIS

Isabella M., NEW JERSEY

Izzy G., VIRGINIA

Jaimee R., FLORIDA

Jane H., FLORIDA

Jenna D., NEW JERSEY

Jess F., NEW JERSEY

Jewel B., NEW JERSEY

Julia B., NEW JERSEY

Julia L., NEW JERSEY

Kaitlyn L., FLORIDA

Kaitlyn L., NEW YORK

Katie M., NEW JERSEY

Katie R., VIRGINIA

Kelly L., MARYLAND

Keren F., NEW JERSEY

Kylie K., NEW JERSEY

Laasya A., OHIO

Laura Y., PENNSYLVANIA

Lauren C., NEW JERSEY

Lauren W., INDIANA

Lexi D., NEW JERSEY

Libby M., ILLINOIS

Lily D., NEW JERSEY

Lily N., NEW YORK

Lily S., DELAWARE

Lindsey B., VIRGINIA

Lola C., NEW JERSEY

Lyla B., NEW YORK

Mahta G., ONTARIO

Makenzie F., CALIFORNIA

Marcella O., VIRGINIA

Marissa J., NEW JERSEY

Maya Y., VIRGINIA

Megan N., ARIZONA

Meghan K., NEW JERSEY

Mei B., ONTARIO

Michelle S., TENNESSEE

Molly M., NEW JERSEY

Naomi P., CALIFORNIA

Nicole N., PENNSYLVANIA

Nora A., NEW YORK

Olivia R., NEW JERSEY

Olivia R., MARYLAND

Olivia S., FLORIDA

Pamela M., VIRGINIA

Paxton K., MARYLAND

Rachel H., VIRGINIA

Rachel S., VIRGINIA

Rebecca Y., INDIA

Riley G., CALIFORNIA

Riley M., NEW JERSEY

Riley S., PENNSYLVANIA

Riya G., NEW JERSEY

Ryan L., NEW YORK

Sabrina G., FLORIDA

Sachi G., NEW JERSEY

Sadie C., VIRGINIA

Samantha R., NEW JERSEY

Sarah K., ALBERTA

Sarah L., NEW JERSEY

Sarah P., DISTRICT OF COLUMBIA

Seerat S., TEXAS

Selin Ö., TURKEY

Shelby B., MARYLAND

Siena P., NEW JERSEY

Skylar L., GEORGIA

Sophia C., VIRGINIA

Sophia R., DISTRICT OF COLUMBIA

Sriya T., NEW JERSEY

Tanvi K., NEW JERSEY

Tapaswini S., INDIA

Taylor B., TORONTO

Tina P., TORONTO

Toujda S., ALGERIA

Unda D., VIRGINIA

Vanessa Q., VIRGINIA

Vasundhara C., INDIA

Winter Noel J., MARYLAND

Yesibel C., NEW YORK

Zareenah A., GEORGIA

Zoe R., NEW YORK

ABOUT ÊTRE

Être is a free mentorship platform for motivated girls. With online resources, after-school clubs, on-site executive events, and virtual mentor pop-ups, Être brings girls directly into companies they choose to meet female leaders face-to-face.

All proceeds of *The Epic Mentor Guide* will go to ensure that every Être event remains free for every girl. Everywhere.

ABOUT THE AUTHOR

Recently named one the first 250 entrepreneurs on the *Forbes* Next 1000 List, Illana Raia is the founder and CEO of Être, a mentorship platform for girls. Believing that mentors matter early, Illana brings girls directly into companies they choose (Spotify, Google, YouTube, NYSE . . .) to meet female leaders face-to-face.

Illana is a member of the International Space Station National Lab Education Subcommittee, serves on the National Girls Collaborative Champions Board, and has authored sixty-plus articles for *HuffPost, Ms.,* and *Thrive Global.* Her award-winning book *Être: Girls, Who Do You Want to Be?* was released on Day of the Girl 2019, featuring wisdom from forty luminary women such as Arianna Huffington, Debra Messing, and Reshma Saujani alongside quotes from fifty girls.

Prior to launching Être in 2016, Illana was a corporate attorney at Skadden Arps in NYC and a guest lecturer at Columbia University. She graduated from Smith College and the University of Chicago Law School and remains unapologetically nerdy.

What kind of mentorship have you found on Wall Street, and did you seek it out or were mentors provided to you?
—Asked at the New York Stock Exchange

What's one thing no one knows about working here?
—Asked at Google

How do you handle it if you are the only woman on a team or in a conference room? Do you care?
—Asked at Morgan Stanley

What's the absolute best part of your job right now?
—Asked at Spotify

What are your tips for producing the best video content, and what's one piece of advice you wish you knew when you started?
—Asked at Billboard